DEDICATION

To Jan Kielanowski and Phil Braude

DEDICATION

To Jan Kielanowski and Phil Braude

PRACTICAL
PIG NUTRITION

C. T. WHITTEMORE
NDA, B Sc, PhD
and
F. W. H. ELSLEY
B Sc, Dip Agric (Cantab), PhD, FI Biol

University of Edinburgh

FARMING PRESS LIMITED
WHARFEDALE ROAD, IPSWICH, SUFFOLK

First published 1976

Second edition (revised) 1977

Second impression (with amendments) 1979

ISBN 0 85236 074 6

© FARMING PRESS LTD 1976

All rights reserved. No part of this publication may be reproduced, stored in a retrieval system, or transmitted, in any form or by any means, electronic, mechanical, photocopying, recording or otherwise, without the prior permission of Farming Press Limited.

Set in ten on eleven point Times and printed in Great Britain on Longbow Cartridge paper by The Leagrave Press Limited, Luton and London, for Farming Press Limited.

CONTENTS

CHAPTER	PAGE

FOREWORD   11
by John R. Luscombe,
Head of Animal Production Department and in charge
of the Pig Husbandry Experimental Station,
Harper Adams Agricultural College.

PREFACE   13

1 OBJECTIVE OF PIG NUTRITION   15

Development of a nutritional program: profit – productivity – individuality – flexibility – humanity – purity – simplicity

2 PIG PRODUCTS   20

Meat: growth – carcase acceptability. The boar: growth to puberty – fertility in the adult boar. Sows: puberty – ovulation – embryonic and foetal development. The litter. Lactation – measuring milk production. Factors affecting milk production: litter size – lactation number – stage of lactation. Piglets. Lifetime production of sows – weight and body composition of sows

3 PROTEINS   39

Digestibility of protein: metabolic faecal losses – particle size and structure – heat damage – inhibitors. Metabolism of digested protein: protein recycling – balance of essential amino acids – amino acid supplementation with synthetic amino acids – non-essential amino acid nitrogen and non-protein nitrogen (NPN) – dietary supply of amino acids – time-base for protein synthesis – biological value. Protein requirements of growing pigs. Protein metabolism in the pregnant sow. Protein requirements of pregnant sows. Protein metabolism in the lactating sow. Protein requirements of lactating sows

4 ENERGY   56

Digestibility of energy. Metabolism of digested energy: maintenance – production – energy from protein – body water – control of body temperature – total energy supply and efficiency – energy requirements of growing pigs. Energy use by pregnant sows: energy requirements of pregnancy. Energy use by lactating sows: energy requirements of lactation

5 MINERALS, VITAMINS AND WATER 73

Minerals. Supplementation of diets – utilisation of the major minerals – sodium and potassium – magnesium – phosphorus and calcium. Vitamins. Fat soluble vitamins: vitamin A – vitamin D – vitamin E – vitamin K. Water soluble vitamins: thiamine – riboflavine – nicotinic acid – pantothenic acid – pyridoxine – cobalamine – choline – biotin – folic acid and inositol – vitamin C. Water. Frequency of provision of water – other uses for water – water allowance

6 APPETITE 88

Diet dilution – stress – sows – frequency of feeding

7 RATIONING 93

Growing pigs: feeding scales – ad libitum – rationing steps – rationing by weight and by time – choice of scale – rationing different sexes – precision. Pregnant sows: flat rate or scale? – the need for weight gain – amount of weight gain. Lactating sows: appetite. Weaned sows for re-breeding. Individual feeding of sows

8 CHOOSING A FEEDING PROGRAM FOR GROWING PIGS—WITH THE HELP OF A MODEL 110

Approaches to predicting pig responses – the way the calculation is made – average responses. Responses particular to individual circumstances: four examples – general level of performance of the model pig – use of results for financial calculations – use of the model to produce targets and in diagnosis

9 CHOOSING A FEEDING PROGRAM FOR THE BREEDING HERD 126

Factors affecting the choice of feeding level: environment – individuality of sows. Distribution of feed in pregnancy and lactation – records. Responses of sows to changes in nutrient supply: feed intake in pregnancy – protein intake in pregnancy – feed intake in lactation – protein intake in lactation – sow liveweight and condition. Choosing a pre-mating feeding program. Choosing a breeding program for breeding boars. Procedure for choosing the feeding program: management – deficiencies – abuses – indicators – action

10 FEEDSTUFFS 145

The metabolism study – metabolism trials. Chemical methods. Tables of feed values. Feeding trials. Unusual feedstuffs – grazing – fibrous feedstuffs

11 DIET FORMULATION 154

Additivity – units of measurement for diet formulation. Hand calculation – some on-farm feed formulation problems – ingredient restraints. Computer calculation – least cost diet formulation: setting up – some practical diets – frequent changes in diet ingredients – the density restraint and unit value of nutrients – high nutrient density diets. How many diets? – simplification – formulating diets with bulky feedstuffs – compensatory protein growth – the weaner pig. Non-nutritional feed additives for growth promotion: feed antibiotics and anti-bacterial agents – copper and arsenicals – hormones – responses

12 IN CONCLUSION 178

Some specific points: individualism – nutritional abuses – using models – husbandry practices – problem variables in the pig – problem variables in the feed – body weight

APPENDICES

Appendix 1	Metabolic body weights	182
Appendix 2	Nutritive values of feeds	183 & 184
Appendix 3	Amino acid composition of proteins in feeds	185
Appendix 4	Some conversions	186

INDEX 187

ILLUSTRATIONS

DIAGRAMS

		PAGE
Fig 2.1.	Increase in lean mass with age	22
Fig 2.2.	Daily rate of gain of lean mass	23
Fig 2.3.	Weight of individual components in the live body of a growing pig fed to a restricted scale	25
Fig 2.4.	Daily gain of individual components of the body of a growing pig fed to a restricted scale	26
Fig 2.5.	Weight increase of foetuses	32
Fig 2.6.	Loss of embryos and foetuses during pregnancy	33
Fig 2.7.	A lactation curve for a sow	36
Fig 2.8.	Growth of piglets with and without creep-feed	37
Fig 3.1-6.	The barrel analogy for amino acid balance	46
Fig 4.1.	Improvement in digestibility following reduction in particle size	60
Fig 4.2.	Reduction in digestibility with increasing fibrousness of diet ingredients	60
Fig 4.3.	Daily gains of energy in the components in the body, and daily losses of energy as heat in the growing pig	62
Fig 4.4.	Effects of increasing daily energy intake upon the efficiency of energy use for growth in the pig	66
Fig 6.1.	Suggested limits to quantity of feed which can be eaten daily by growing pigs	89
Fig 6.2.	Possible limits to the energy intake (DE) of growing pigs	89
Fig 6.3.	Energy and feed intake control in pigs	90
Fig 7.1.	Examples of weight-based ration scales for growing pigs	94
Fig 7.2.	The effect of pregnancy ration upon the birth-weight of piglets	103
Fig 7.3.	Example of weight changes during the reproductive cycle of sows	107
Fig 8.1.	Responses to level of feeding (ration scale) by growing pigs with three different maximum limits to their daily rate of protein deposition	115
Fig 8.2.	Responses to house temperature by growing pigs given three ration scales	117

Fig 8.3.	Responses of growing pigs according to weight at slaughter and diet	118
Fig 8.4.	Responses of growing pigs to concentration of dietary protein of three biological values	120
Fig 8.5.	Responses to concentration of dietary protein by growing pigs with different maximum limits to their daily rate of protein deposition	121
Fig 8.6.	Responses to concentration of dietary protein in diets with different energy densities	123
Fig 9.1.	Maximum and minimum levels of energy intakes by sows	127
Fig 9.2.	Maximum and minimum levels of digestible crude protein intakes by sows	127
Fig 9.3.	Effects of feed intake in pregnancy on sow productivity	134
Fig 9.4.	Effects of protein intake in pregnancy on sow productivity	136
Fig 9.5.	Effects of feed intake in lactation on milk yield and liveweight losses	137
Fig 9.6.	Effects of protein intake in lactation on liveweight losses	139
Fig 9.7.	Effects of feed intake in pregnancy upon the birth-weight of piglets on three separate farms	143
Fig 10.1.	Measurements for a metabolism study	146
Fig 10.2.	Metabolism crate for growing pigs	147

PHOTOGRAPHS

Pig Products:
1. Boar sperm — 28
2. Milk — 28
3. Weaners — 29
4. Carcase meat — 29

Rations:
5. Young growers are often fed ad lib — 98
6. Fattening pigs are usually rationed to a scale according to weight or age — 98
7. Individual feeding allows ration control for pregnant sows — 99
8. Group feeding, with the sow to the rear in trouble — 99
9. Group housing, but individual feeding — 99

Sow Condition in Late Pregnancy:
10. Too thin — 132
11. About right — 132
12. A little too fat — 132

Sow Condition:
13. Milking off her back — 133
14. Much too thin – 'the thin sow syndrome' — 133

Feeding:
15. Grazing can provide 6 MJ DE, or none — 157
16. Mill and mix unit with a throughput of 2 tonne/hour — 157

FOREWORD

by JOHN R. LUSCOMBE

*Head of Animal Production Department and in charge
of the Pig Husbandry Experimental Station,
Harper Adams Agricultural College*

THE MOTTO of the Royal Agricultural Society, *Practice with Science*, is one which we should at all times attempt to put into operation. Unfortunately there are few people sufficiently conversant with both aspects to qualify for the role of advisers or leaders, thus enabling the motto to be followed effectively. However, I have no hesitation in including the authors of this book among the few possessing these dual qualities.

It is most refreshing to find that a 'new approach' has been adopted. After a precise but nevertheless easily read account of the science of pig nutrition, suggestions are put forward regarding the application of this to feeding. 'One pig's meal is another pig's poison' is a true statement, as evidenced by a particular feeding regime being eminently successful on one unit but a disaster on another.

As food accounts for eighty per cent of pigmeat production costs, how very vital is a thorough knowledge of the subject. A study of *Practical Pig Nutrition* will enable a pig feeder to interpret and put into practice the best system for his herd.

The book is an excellent distillation and blend of scientific knowledge and applied feeding presented in such a way as to be comprehensible to a very wide readership.

For scientists, advisers, lecturers and students, it should be on the bookshelf but not allowed to get dusty.

JOHN R. LUSCOMBE

Newport, Salop
December, 1975

PREFACE

THE THEME of this book is choice. In the fluctuating environment of pig business, only by flexibility can the market system be exploited by pig producers and feed compounders; we would wish the pig producer and pig feeder to be the masters of the system and not its servants.

The practice of recommending 'best' feeding programs for pigs largely eliminates flexibility and has been rejected. If choice is the theme, those choosing must base their decisions on objective information. We have tried to supply some of that information.

An attempt has been made to distinguish between what is open to manipulation by man and what is rather more a constant of the biology of the pig. To help in this distinction, some of the known science of nutrition and growth has been described. The background to least-cost diet formulation and nutritional evaluation is included so as to highlight their limitations as well as emphasising their benefits. The book has been prepared in the hope that it will contribute to a change in attitude and action with regard to diet formulation and to the practical decisions in the choice of pig-feeding programs. In this respect, we are reminded of a prayer attributed to Reinhold Niebuhr which asks for 'Serenity to accept what cannot be changed, courage to change what should be changed, and wisdom to distinguish the one from the other'.

The work of a great number of scientists and farmers has contributed to the content of this book by way of research findings and practical experience. In the case of CTW, acknowledgment is made to his family and relations, whose running of a production unit and whose philosophies of pig-keeping, figure largely in that author's experience. Similarly, FWHE has greatly depended on the experience and wisdom of his friends in agriculture, who have invariably anticipated the results of research.

We have drawn heavily on the work of our colleagues at universities, colleges and research institutes; in particular those from the University of Edinburgh, the East of Scotland College of Agriculture and the Institute of Animal Physiology and Nutrition, Jablonna, Warsaw.

For the graphics we thank Mr Gordon Finnie, who was also

responsible for most of the photographs. Dr R. H. F. Hunter supplied photograph No. 1 and *Pig Farming* Nos. 4, 5 and 15.

COLIN T. WHITTEMORE

FRANK W. H. ELSLEY

Edinburgh
October, 1975

Chapter 1

OBJECTIVE OF PIG NUTRITION

PIG PRODUCTION should satisfy two objectives; the supply of meat to the human population and the supply of profit to the producer. The nutritional aspect of pig production is both the major proportion of production costs, and the major means by which the production system can be manipulated. Nutrition is *not* for satisfying any inborn requirements of pigs for particular quantities of food. Nutrition *is* for creating and controlling growth and reproduction, such that it satisfies the requirements of the producer for profit, and mankind for meat.

Pig nutrition should be under the control of the pig producer, not the nutritionist; and each producer has different objectives for his pigs. There are as many ways of feeding pigs as there are producers. Not only does each producer find himself in a unique position regarding the strategy he should adopt to feed his pigs, but the circumstances of the outside world demand that he continually reappraises his position. Most profitable production cannot be maintained with static feeding policies in a changing environment. Information given to producers by nutritionists should therefore allow for these two facets of pig production; the individuality of producers and the changing nature of the markets which supply feedstuffs to the industry and receive carcase meat from it.

There can be distrust of the views of scientists who propose complicated and impractical systems of nutrition. This distrust has protected many producers from a number of rather expensive suggestions, but it has also precluded them from adopting some more sensible nutritional ideas which would have resulted in a greater profit. Conversely, there are those who have advocated the pre-eminence of the practical husbandry view as a means of promulgating ideas about pig nutrition. This has resulted in the erection of practical feeding systems, which although obviously successful under certain circumstances, cannot be transplanted readily to a range of different circumstances. One of the problems with interpreting nutritional information into a husbandry system is that the husbandry *system* itself becomes the information, rather than the *nutrition*. Thus, it is the system which is advocated and not the original nutritional information which led to its successful development. Such systems become ossified, and the basic nutritional principles which originally led to their successful development are neglected.

An historical examination of practical advice would reveal that those who advocate particular feeding practices based on commercial examples have been no more correct in the past than the 'ivory tower' scientists.

The reader will find that there are some unexpected absentees from the chapters which follow; those seeking assertive statements about the nutrient needs of pigs will not find them; those who wish a compendium of scientific information on pig production must look elsewhere; there is little reiteration of other scientists' proven findings.

Although the debt owed by the whole pig industry to nutritional scientists is acknowledged, it was considered that a catalogue of experimental findings was not the best way to do justice to the vast amount of effort which has gone into the elucidation of our present state of knowledge. Rather the research findings of the last thirty years have been incorporated into a nutritional philosophy that is **based on physiology and biochemistry, but which is rigorously** directed towards practical pig management and realistic views of the reasons why farmers keep pigs and the problems they encounter.

It is possible that the science of animal nutrition will, over the next few years, move from an era of patient exploratory experimentation into one of simulation, model building and computerisation. This point is not yet reached, but some of the concepts expressed in this book try to make a step in that direction. Fortunately, it is not necessary for one to be indubitably right, merely that one progresses in what is probably a forward direction, and that one is a little less wrong today than one was yesterday.

Freedom of action

If there is a theme to the book it is one of choice, freedom of action and flexibility. The reader's attention is drawn to those factors in the production system and in the basic physiology of the animal which simply cannot be changed, or which are only changed at one's peril. Here, adversity must be turned to advantage, if these facets of the system are to be exploited. Conversely, there are other factors, vital to efficient and profitable production, which are very readily manipulated. The more information that is available about these, the more fruitful are likely to be one's pig-feeding stratagems.

Other sources of information

The book has been prepared in full knowledge of two others from the same publishers; these are *Early Weaning of Pigs* by G. Brent, D. Hovell, R. F. Ridgeon, and W. J. Smith, and *Practical Pig Production* by Keith Thornton. Detailed discussion of those areas which were admirably covered by these authors has therefore been avoided. A third book *Swine Production in Temperate and Tropical Environments* by W. G. Pond and J. H. Maner, published by W. H. Freeman & Co., San Francisco, contains a wealth of information about feedstuffs. In recognition of this, the nutritive values of feeds have been presented in simple tabular form.

Weights and measures

In accord with the general moves towards metrication in agriculture, the text uses metric units. Occasionally, imperial units are also given, and a short conversion table is given at the end of the book in Appendix 4.

DEVELOPMENT OF A NUTRITIONAL PROGRAM

The most important problems which face the pig manager are those regarding the nutrition of his pigs. Decisions about nutrition can only be properly made when there is adequate information available. Heresay, intuition or the general rule are not good enough.

Profit

Most farmers keep pigs for profit. Despite this, nutritional requirements are not usually presented in terms of the profit they may engender. In general, the nutritionists have difficulty in supplying hard numerical data about the way pigs react to nutrients. These data are needed by management before any monetary value can be attached to the various nutritional inputs and outputs. Only after the monetary aspect has been included can the financial benefits of various courses of action be compared.

Productivity

Productivity is usually regarded as an input function, maximising by providing the best possible combination of the highest quality inputs. High productivity is, however, little related to profitability. Further, many production objectives are mutually cancelling; faster growing pigs usually grade less well.

Some items of production information are more useful than others. Manipulation of a system in a positive manner requires the fullest possible information about the system concerned. Production data are vital to planning nutritional policies. Such information would include: number of piglets reared to weaning per sow per year, rate of sow culling, number of sows on a unit at any one time which are neither pregnant (as shown by a negative three-week return) nor lactating, age of pigs at slaughter, weight at slaughter, and grade.

The use of production *targets* is likely to be unhelpful, because generalised targets fail to account for individual circumstances. Before any sensible judgments can be made about a unit's productivity in relation to a production target, the 'production' concerned must be evaluated in monetary and not biological terms. The fact that 90 per cent of pigs from a unit grade A1 is only relevant if the profit is A1 as well. It can be the case that the penalties in terms of feed costs far outweigh the benefits of the price differential for grade.

Individuality

The authoritarian view of pig production is not only inappropriate, but it is likely to be wrong. Having no National pigs, National pig farms or National pig farmers, there can be no nationally applicable pig-feeding plan. The desire to produce a National pig-feeding plan is quite a common syndrome; it may be found in every article which recommends this or that nutrient regime. The fact that many units may use the same breed of pig or the same housing system does not justify the assumption that a feeding system can be standardised.

If account is to be taken of the individuality of production units, the ways in which units are individual must be quantified with adequate records. Where there are no records, differences between units cannot be allowed for and there is no alternative to the 'National Plan'.

Flexibility

That a system has proved successful in the past is only likely to ensure its success in the future if circumstances don't change. Brief recollection of prices for feedstuffs and returns for pork and bacon pigs, over say a two-year period is sufficient evidence that circumstances *do* change—dramatically. The pig production system, and particularly its nutritional aspects, must be able to respond, and respond quickly, to market forces.

Humanity

Agriculture serves the human population. Its customers are simultaneously growing further away from the land whilst concerning themselves evermore in its affairs. The incursion of the 'public conscience' in pig production is likely to get greater, not less. Fortunately, most practices which are unacceptable from the welfare aspect are also likely to be unprofitable in the long term. However, it is possible that a reassessment of animal welfare by the general public may require a reassessment of nutritional well-being. There may be some question, for example, about the well-being of pregnant sows given small quantities of low-fibre diets.

Purity
The pig industry competes at two levels. Firstly, there is competition with other animals and with plants; these being alternatives to pigs as a means for the production of protein for human consumption. Secondly, where countries trade in meat, pigs produced in one country compete with pigs from another. For example, in the United Kingdom home-produced pigmeat competes with that imported from other EEC countries.

To be competitive, all possible advantage must be extracted from whatever potentially beneficial aids are available. On the other hand, one must beware that the image of the wholesomeness of pigmeat is not lost by adverse public reaction to specific components of pig production systems.

Pigmeat must be produced to satisfy the visible criteria of fatness and acceptability. These quality controls are applied at the abattoir by grade schemes and meat inspection procedures. But pigmeat must also satisfy the invisible criteria of palatability and freedom from taints, odour, residues or contaminants. The utilisation of some nutritional feed ingredients and all feed-additives may come to be viewed more in these terms than in terms of the potential improvement in efficiency which might accrue in the short term.

Simplicity
The benefits of simplicity are self evident, although sometimes in order to come to the right simple solution it is necessary to pursue a complex argument. Nevertheless, we hope that the reader will be persuaded that a careful and comprehensive assessment of nutritional problems in pig production can be rewarded by simple practical solutions.

Chapter 2

PIG PRODUCTS

MEAT

PIGMEAT IS produced as a result of pig growth. As nutrition controls growth, the meat-producing function is closely controlled by manipulation of the feeding regime. The way in which growth is controlled by means of the dietary inputs governs the cost of the diet, the efficiency of food use, the quality of the end-product and the final return for the carcase.

A range of possible performances by three pigs when fed differently is shown in Table 2.1. The regimes which brought about these remarkable differences in growth rate, feed efficiency and fatness are discussed later.

TABLE 2.1. Performance of 3 pigs (A, B & C)

Pig	Start weight (kg)	Finish weight (kg)	Growth rate (g/day)	Feed/gain (F.C.R.)	P_2 fat depth measurement (mm)
A	20	100	361	4·2	20
B	20	100	900	2·8	30
C	20	100	550	2·8	20

The composition of a 100 kg pig is given in Table 2.2. The content of the alimentary tract (given as 5 kg) will obviously depend on the size of the previous meal, and the time between eating and weighing. Upon slaughter the pig is bled, the bristles removed, and the intestines and offals withdrawn. Some of the offals (liver, kidney) are eaten; most are not. The carcase is about 73 per cent of the liveweight, but still contains the skeleton and has the head, skin and trotters attached. The edible meat portion is about 55 per cent of liveweight and comprises tissues which are fat and those which are muscle (or lean). The fat and lean can be separated physically, but even then, fat contains some lean and lean contains some fat. For the present purposes lean is assumed to contain 75–80 per cent water and fat 9–12 per cent water. The total chemical composition of the body is

TABLE 2.2. Simplified guide to the composition of a 100 kg pig

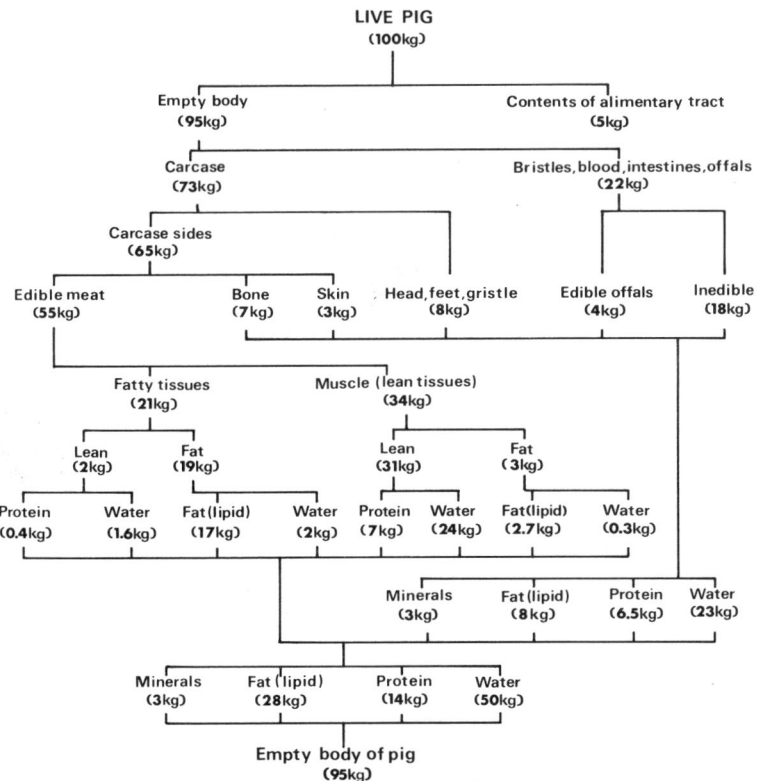

determined by gathering together the chemical composition of all the components, and this is shown at the foot of the table; about 3 kg minerals, 28 kg fat, 14 kg protein and 50 kg water.

When considering growth from the nutritional point of view it is convenient to work initially with the chemical components; minerals, fat, protein, and water. Next, the chemical composition is translated into fatness and carcass quality.

When the pig grows edible meat-protein, it also grows skin-protein, intestine-protein, lung-protein and so on. The efficiency of dietary protein use for these various purposes is unlikely to be very different, but the financial rewards for meat protein are very much greater than those for skin or intestine. Unfortunately, there is little opportunity for directing feed protein into one body function rather than another; indeed, although the intestine, for example, is not valuable in a pig's carcase, the pig needs it when it is alive.

Both lean (muscle) growth and fat growth are open to control by nutritional means. There is, however, an upper limit to lean growth; this need not necessarily always be achieved, but it cannot be exceeded. Because the objective is generally maximisation of lean, the tendency is to feed to the upper limits of lean growth.

Any such limit which the pig might have in respect to fat growth is far above the tolerance of consumers of bacon and pork; the object is therefore to control the fat fraction of growth within the context of optimisation of financial returns. It is largely the relationship between dietary regime and fatness which governs the financial success of a pigmeat production enterprise.

Minimum fatness is *not* the objective; profit lies in *manipulating* the rate of fat growth to find the optimum combinations of diet, feed efficiency, growth rate, and carcase quality. This optimum is unlikely to be commensurate with minimum fat and is also sure to change just as frequently as changes in the price of diet ingredients and returns for pig carcases.

GROWTH

All animals possess the target of an ultimate, or mature, body weight. Growth is the animal's endeavour to reach that target. The concept of a 'mature size' probably relates to the mass of *lean* at maturity, the fat mass being notoriously variable in animals of similar maturity.

Animals appear to have some sense of chronology, thus they are propelled to the goal of maturity both by weight and by time. If, of two pigs, one is destined to have a larger mature lean mass, but both have the same chronological scale for age at maturity, the one with the larger mature mass must eat more and grow faster. It follows that

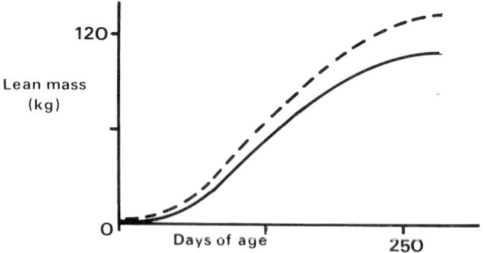

Figure 2.1. Increase in lean mass with age.

a likely outcome of selection for higher growth rate is greater mature size.

The solid line in Figure 2.1 represents the rate of accumulation of lean in a pig up to maturity. A pig with a greater mature lean mass is represented by the broken line which, of necessity, has a steeper slope indicating faster growth to reach a greater weight in the same time. The figure also shows how, providing the nutrition is satisfactory, the rate of lean gain in the pig is remarkably constant over the weight range 20–120 kg (45–260 lb); the 'cruising speed' for protein synthesis being reached early in life and only tailing off as the animal approaches maturity.

Lean largely consists of protein and water. The amount of water which is associated with protein in lean tissue is, however, not constant. In a 20 kg pig there is about 80 per cent water in the lean (fat free) tissues, at 70 kg 78 per cent, and at 120 kg 76 per cent.

Lean growth is depicted as a daily rate in Figure 2.2. For the major part of growth from 20 to 120 kg this daily rate is practically constant. The nature of daily lean growth is controversial. Although a number of serial slaughter experiments have confirmed the general nature of the pattern shown in Figure 2.2, the picture is confused by

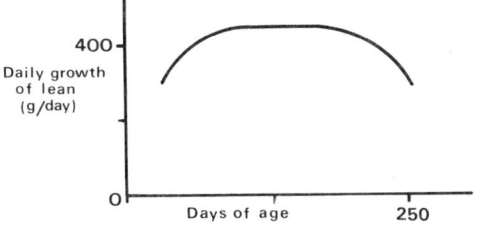

Figure 2.2. Daily rate of gain of lean mass.

the possibility that protein growth could be held back by nutritional rather than physiological factors. For the present, however, it may be taken that the daily rate of protein growth and of lean gain is relatively constant.

The daily rate of protein growth and the limit to that daily rate is crucial to every aspect of feeding pigs. Upon it depends the appropriate specification for the pig's diet, the amount of the diet to be rationed, the efficiency of growth and the quality of the final product. Some values for maximum rates of protein deposition have been proposed and are given in Table 2.3.

Fat deposition does not behave like lean growth. The prime

controller of fat growth is not maturity, or time, but energy intake. Dietary energy supplied in excess of the animal's immediate need is channelled into fat deposition.

TABLE 2.3. Maximum daily rates of protein and lean deposition (g/day)

Pig	Protein	Lean*
Unimproved	80	350
Improved	120	530
Gilt	120	530
Castrate	90	400
Boar	140	610

*Total lean deposition as given here relates to whole body lean and not carcase dissected lean tissue which commonly ranges between 200 and 350 g/day.

Nevertheless, it is probably as well to consider fat as being of two types, because it seems that not all fat is simply a depot for the accumulation of surplus energy. When the composition of the growth of pigs is examined, even under the most adverse nutritional regimes protein deposition is invariably accompanied by at least an equal quantity of fat. This pattern of deposition would give rise to a tissue composition of around 18 per cent protein: 18 per cent fat: 64 per cent water, which represents 80 per cent lean: 20 per cent fat.

If the concept of a minimum need for fat is accepted, then the remaining fraction of fat growth can be considered as being wholly dependent upon the extent to which food energy is supplied surplus to the need of all the various other body functions. The level of fatness is thus largely, but not totally, a function of the amount of food which the animal eats.

The increase in the weight of the various body components with age and liveweight is shown in Figure 2.3. This figure shows how increase in ash is fairly constant. Ash remains at about 3 per cent of the total body over the whole growth phase. Protein comprises about 15 per cent of the total body weight; rather more in the younger pig and rather less in the older pig. The growth of fat continues ever faster as the pig increases in size, and accounts for 10 per cent of the body of the young 10 kg pig and 30 per cent of the body of the 100 kg fattener. The figure refers to pigs fed to a restricted scale; had they been given more food the increase in fat growth would have been even more dramatic, each additional kilo of feed producing 200 g or so of fat. Conversely, a more restricted scale of feeding would have reduced fat growth to less than that shown in Figure 2.3, the degree of reduction relating to the severity of feed restriction.

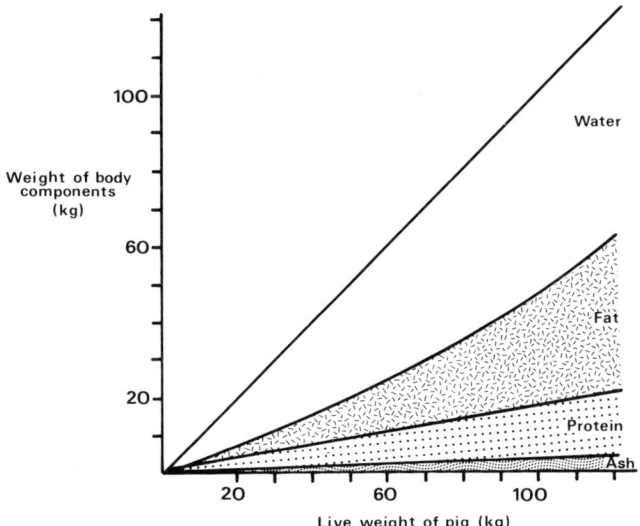

Figure 2.3. Weight of individual components in the live body of a growing pig fed to a restricted scale.

Figure 2.4 (page 26) shows the daily growth of the pig. Again, the figure relates to a pig given a restricted level of feeding such as might be found in commercial practice. As the pig ages and becomes heavier the rate of daily liveweight gain increases—from about 400 g at 20 kg, to 800 g at 100 kg. As the rate of gain increases then so does the proportion of that gain which is fat. Because the rate of protein deposition is fairly constant, after 40 kg in the present example, it follows that any growth rate increase can only come from additional increments of fat.

The increase in growth rate that occurs as the animal increases in size is therefore primarily fat deposition. Any increase in growth to be had in terms of the daily rate is also primarily fat. As a rule, the maximum rate of lean growth for an average pig is about 450 g daily. Any daily gain in liveweight greater than 450 g can be assumed to be fat—the greater the gain the more the fat. The composition of gains below 550 g daily will adhere to the 1:1 protein fat rule and be in the region of 80 g lean to 20 g fat in each 100 g of gain.

The importance of water in the composition of the body and of the daily gain is exemplified in both Figures 2.3 and 2.4. The greater part of this water is associated with protein in the form of lean tissue (muscle). Although fat growth outpaces protein growth at all stages except when the animal is very young, the growth of fat only approaches a rate equal to that of lean in the final stages of fattening. The ratio of protein to fat in the gain of a 10 kg pig is about 1:1, the ratio of protein to fat in the gain of a 100 kg pig is usually about 1:4. Thus, as pigs become heavier the amount of food needed to maintain the animal rises and the proportion of fat in the gain increases.

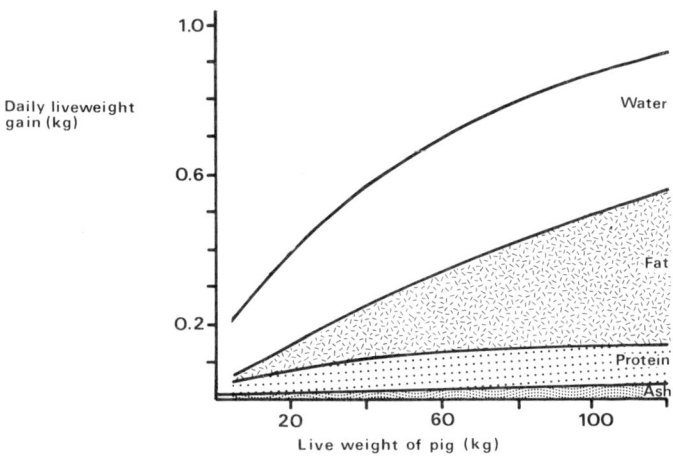

Figure 2.4. Daily gain of individual components of the body of a growing pig fed to a restricted scale.

Because the water in animal tissues is associated with protein, and water needs no food for its deposition in the body, the use of feed for growth becomes less efficient as the animal grows older and fatter. This happens both on account of maintenance costs and on account of fat in the gain. Feed conversion efficiency (kg feed/kg gain) worsens from about 2:1 in the 20 kg pig to 4:1 in the 100 kg pig. This situation should not be interpreted as also meaning that increased rate of growth by fat growth is always inefficient. Quite the contrary; as the maintenance loading becomes greater it is all the more important to keep up the growth rate to defray maintenance costs. Slow growth can be even more inefficient than fat growth.

CARCASE ACCEPTABILITY

After the pig has been slaughtered and eviscerated, meat inspection procedures ensure that the meat is wholesome and fit for human consumption. Next, measurements are taken to determine the price that will be paid. The important measurements are weight and backfat thickness. The determination of backfat, particularly at mid-back over the eye muscle with an introscope probe (the P_2 measurement) is simple and quick. There is generally a reasonable relationship between P_2 fat depth and the amount of fat in the carcase as a whole.

Apart from fat content, other aspects of eating quality in pigmeat are not assessed and do not enter into the determination of quality or grade for purposes of payment. Neither is eating quality much affected by the nutrition which the pig receives. Changes in the amount of food eaten, or the proportion of protein in the diet, will affect the lean-to-fat ratio of the **meat; but apart** from its effect on fatness, not the tenderness, colour, texture, juiciness or flavour. Occasionally some off-flavour in feedstuffs, particularly in oils, may be transferred to the fat of pigmeat. But this problem is specific to some feedstuffs with a high content of distinctly flavoured oil (for example, some fish products), or feeds which have been improperly treated.

THE BOAR

Growth to puberty

Puberty in both males and females is related to age and to weight. Given satisfactory nutrition, it is unusual for animals not to reach puberty at around the expected age, or to be incapable subsequently of normal reproduction.

The boar reaches puberty, as judged by development of the male organs, between 125 days and 170 days, although the capacity to breed is usually not achieved before 150 days when the boar weighs between 80 and 110 kg liveweight. At 130 days of age, the total amount of ejaculate may be 100 ml and the number of motile sperm 10×10^9. By two years of age sperm production has increased to about 130 ml and 33×10^9 motile sperm.

Most examples of infertility and poor production of motile sperm by young boars have resulted from extremely low levels of feeding, particularly in the month prior to use. Restoration of adequate nutrition usually leads to normal reproductive activity and capacity after a period of repletion.

Excessively high levels of nutrition up to puberty can reduce the long-term productivity of boars. Extremely high growth rates up to 70 of 80 kg liveweight have been suspected as causing deformities such as leg weaknesses. In addition, boars which are heavy in respect of age and which are fat may lack libido and produce small ejaculates at low sperm quality.

Continued on page 30

PRODUCTS

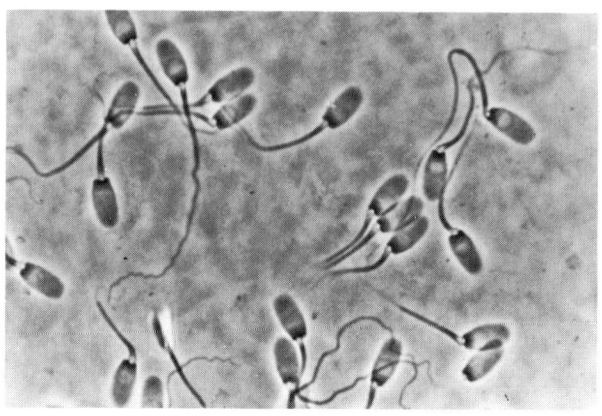

1. Boar sperm.

2. Milk.

3. Weaners.

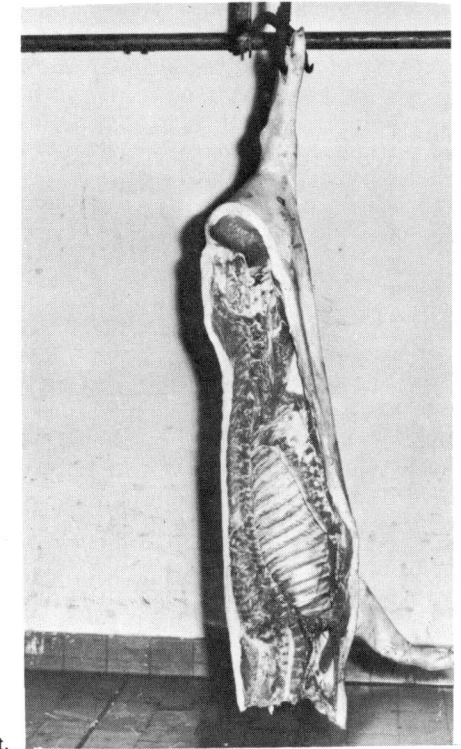

4. Carcase meat.

continued from page 27

Fertility in the adult boar

The nutrient requirements for semen production are minute in comparison with the requirements for maintaining the boar in good health. If the animal is in reasonable body condition and receiving a conventional pig diet, cases of low semen production are unlikely to have resulted from any deficiency of the major nutrients or of trace minerals and vitamins.

If the animal is in good health and suffering no clinical or subclinical disease syndrome, then reproductive failure through lack of libido or reduced sperm production is usually associated with over-fatness or with over-use.

SOWS

The object in the breeding herd is high productivity for the lowest possible cost; in particular, the costs of sow feeding must be minimised. To balance productivity with production costs, it is necessary to impose control over those aspects of reproduction which are open to manipulation by nutrition.

Many of the factors which are crucial to sow productivity are more influenced by aspects of management such as housing conditions, environment, disease, and behaviour, than by variation in the quality or quantity of feed eaten. In some circumstances, good nutrition can mitigate the effects of, say, an adverse environment. But it is preferable to modify those aspects of management which limit productivity rather than to attempt to ameliorate their effects by nutritional means.

PUBERTY

Sexual maturity in gilts occurs at around 180 days of age, when they should weigh 70–100 kg. This age is modified by level of nutrition and by liveweight. Faster growing animals will reach puberty a little (10–15 days) earlier. Conversely, feed intakes of below 2 kg, associated with weight stasis or weight loss in the gilts, may delay first heat by up to 30 days. Obesity, on the other hand, may have the effect of reducing reproductive performance of gilts. Because of the influence of age, gilts fed generously will be heavier and fatter at puberty than those fed to a more restrictive scale. If gilts are to be grown fast, either a heavier weight of breeding animal must be accepted, or the gilt given extra encouragement to reach puberty at an earlier age. Gilts are often not mated at first heat (oestrus), and the target weight for first conception varies, according to circumstances, from 90–115 kg.

At any given weight, the faster grown gilt will be younger and likely to have exhibited fewer heat cycles prior to service. The number of eggs released from the ovary increases up to the third heat after puberty, and gilts which are heavier and older at puberty also shed more ova than younger, lighter gilts. Whether or not ovulation rate brings about any concommitant increase in the number of piglets which are actually born is another matter.

Age at first heat is also influenced by breed, social environment and management; 180 days (± 10 days) is the average under British conditions for the Landrace and Large White breeds. A number of management procedures can help to make the signs of heat more obvious, and reinforce the oestrus behaviour of the gilt. This facilitates early reproduction and reduces the incidence of 'silent heats'. Procedures include: penning the gilts away from boars, followed by his strategic introduction when a potentially 'silent heat' is thought to be due; moving the gilts from one pen to another or transporting them in a lorry; mixing with other females; or reducing feed intake for a few days.

OVULATION

Ova are released 36–42 hours after the external symptoms of oestrus occur, and this release can itself take up to four hours. The extent to which ovulation can be stimulated is a matter of debate but the act of mating appears to accelerate the time of ovulation. Only about 60 per cent of the ova released result in the birth of viable piglets. Mature sows usually release 16–18 ova at each heat, the number rising slightly with each succeeding litter.

Normal ovulation does not usually occur whilst the sow is lactating and the oestrus which may be seen in early lactation is usually non-ovulatory. Oestrus can occur if milk production is low or if the pigs are removed from the sow for up to 12 hours per day at around the 21st day.

EMBRYONIC AND FOETAL DEVELOPMENT

Immediately following fertilisation the ovum starts drawing on the fluids of the uterus for nutrient supply. By day 11 the ovum begins to attach and implant in the lining of the uterus, by day 18 the placenta is functioning and by the 28th day the foetus is 1·0–1·5 g in weight. **The weight then increases rapidly (see Figure 2.5) so that the foetuses weigh 50 g on the 50th day, 220 g on the 70th day, 600 g on the 90th day and 1000–1300 g by the 114th day.**

The membranes which surround the foetus from an early age are **crucial to both the nutrient exchange and the passage of excretary**

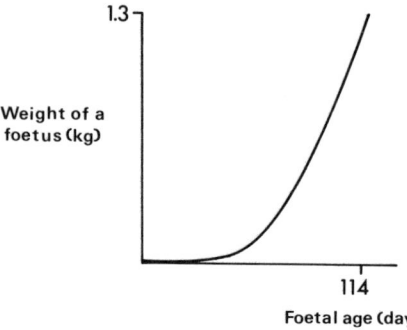

Figure 2.5. Weight increase of foetuses.

products between the sow and the foetuses. They also act as short-term stores of the nutrients to be released at later stages as the foetuses require them. These membranes reach their maximum weight of about 2·5 kg by the 70th day, and thereafter remain constant.

The amniotic and allantoic fluids which surround the foetuses also reach a maximum weight of about 6 kg at 70 days and thereafter decline up to parturition. These fluids, quite apart from physically protecting the foetuses, also act as a mineral bank and as a store of by-products of foetal metabolism such as urea and creatinine.

At term, there are about 13 kg of piglets, 2·5 kg membranes, 2 kg fluids and the maternal uterus has increased in weight from about 1 to 4 kg.

Considering the range of piglet birth-weights, the composition of the pigs at birth at any specified birth-weight is remarkably constant, see Table 2.4. Foetal pigs are unusual in that they have a very low content of fat (lipid), but a high level of carbohydrate in the form of glycogen. This provides the piglet after birth with a readily available

TABLE 2.4. Composition of piglets at birth[1] and to 20 kg, together with expected age and daily liveweight gains

	Water (%)	Lipid (%)	Protein (%)	Ash (%)	Expected age (days)	Weight gain (g/day)
Birth (1·25 kg)	81	1·0	11	4	—	—
5 kg	68	12	13	3	22	240
10 kg	66	15	14	3	39	320
15 kg	64	18	15	3	53	380
20 kg	63	18	15	3	65	500

[1] In addition to water, lipid, protein and ash, the new-born pig contains 2·5 per cent of glycogen.

source of energy for the first few days of life until dietary sources of energy (from milk) are available in sufficient quantity.

The total amount of nutrients stored in the products of conception (that is, the foetuses, fluids and membranes) is low relative to the total intake of nutrients by the sow. It has been suggested that the foetuses of mammals are accorded a priority in the relative distribution of circulatory nutrients in the body of pregnant females. It is rather that, over most of pregnancy, foetal demands are a low and relatively insignificant proportion of circulatory blood nutrients. Whilst it is true that the placenta ensures nutrient supply to the foetuses and buffers them against short-term fluctuations, it is not the case that foetuses have absolute priority for nutrients. Absolute priority would mean that foetal growth is independent of food intake by the sow—which clearly cannot be the case. As evidenced in Figure 2.5, the rate of foetal growth from 80–110 days is very rapid. This growth places ever increasing demands upon the maternal body, and birth weight *can* be influenced at this time by the nutrient supply to the foetuses from dietary sources and/or from maternal body stores.

THE LITTER

The greatest single factor in the determination of growth of individual foetuses is the number of foetuses in the uterus.

Why there should be such a wide range in litter size is not understood. Figure 2.6 shows how about 40 per cent of potential embryos and foetuses are lost before parturition; 5–10 per cent of ova

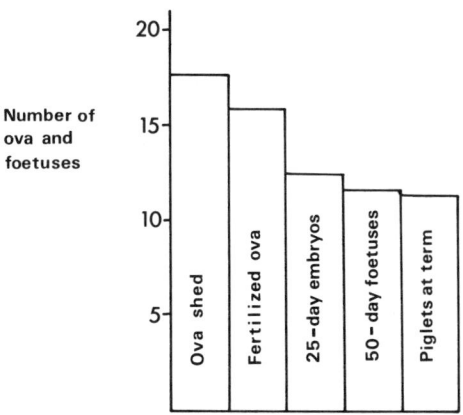

Figure 2.6. Loss of embryos and foetuses during pregnancy.

are lost within two days of release from the ovary. The main losses, which are embryos, can be higher than 33 per cent. After the 25th day loss rate is usually low.

Increases in ovulation rate to above about 20 ova do not usually result in increases in litter size. This may be due to the sow having a limited uterine capacity, which ensures that by day 50 not more than a certain number of embryos (often about 10–16) are alive. This process, although general, is not absolute; sows sometimes produce up to 20 piglets in a single litter. Limited uterine capacity may also explain the finding that larger litters contain more small piglets; there being an inverse relationship between litter size and average individual piglet birthweight.

The ability of a sow to produce litters with large numbers of pigs is poorly inherited and the possibility of increasing litter size by selection is not promising. On the other hand, there are differences of two piglets or more per litter between breeds; as exemplified by a comparison of Poland China and Duroc with Large White and Landrace breeds.

LACTATION

Interest in early weaning of pigs has raised the question as to whether lactation in the sow is a desirable or essential component of sow management. However exciting the recent developments in early weaning, it is unlikely that a significant proportion of litters will be weaned earlier than 21 days of age, and the majority of piglets in Western Europe will be weaned between four and six weeks of age. Milk production of the sow will therefore continue to be an important determinant of piglet growth, particularly in the period up to 21 days of age.

Measuring milk production

The milk production of a sow is as much a function of the vigour of the piglets in removing the milk from the mammary glands as of the synthesis of milk by the sow. Total milk consumed by the piglets can only be satisfactorily measured by weighing the piglets before and after they have suckled. As can readily be envisaged, data collected by this means are subject to considerable error.

FACTORS AFFECTING MILK PRODUCTION

Litter size

As shown in Table 2.5 the number of pigs in the litter can greatly influence both total yield and the milk consumed by individual piglets. This clearly demonstrates that if a feeding system is to allow for the rate of milk production, it should take into account the litter size. Although this is frequently advocated, it is infrequently practiced.

TABLE 2.5. Yield of milk by sows as influenced by number of pigs in the litter

Number of piglets in litter	Milk yield of sow (kg/day)	Milk intake of piglets (kg/pig/day)
6	5-6	1·0
8	6-7	0·9
10	7-8	0·8
12	8-9	0·7

Lactation number

It is evident from Table 2.6 that the milk yield of sows increases considerably between the first and second lactation, although this is due in part to second litter sows suckling more pigs. The differences between the lactations are largely in total yield and changes in the composition of the milk are fairly small. However, fat percentage does tend to decline in the third lactation and this can be attributed to declining fat reserves in the sow.

TABLE 2.6. Yield of milk by sows as influenced by lactation number

Lactation number	Milk yield (kg/day)
1st	5-6
2nd	7-8
3rd	7-8

Stage of lactation

The yield and composition of milk alters during the course of lactation; Figure 2.7 (p. 36) shows how milk yield reaches a peak between the second and fourth week. The lactation curves of individual sows vary greatly, and there are also differences between the lactation curves of different breeds.

The percentage composition in terms of protein, fat, lactose, and ash changes with stage of lactation. The daily production of lactose and fat decline as lactation proceeds whilst the daily production of milk protein remains relatively constant up to eight weeks.

The pattern of milk yield in the lactation indicates that the sow's nutrient needs for milk production diminish after the 5–6th week of lactation. If the ration regime is constant over the whole lactation, the sow weaned at eight weeks has the opportunity to replace depleted body stores in late lactation. Sows which are weaned at the peak of lactation have no such opportunity, and their body reserves are likely to be correspondingly more depleted.

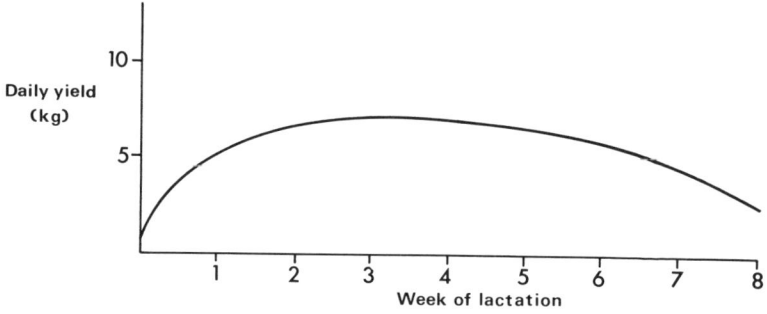

Figure 2.7. A lactation curve for a sow.

PIGLETS

Piglets grow on both mother's milk and on supplementary feed (creep feed). Usually, piglets are offered creep feed from about seven days of age to supplement the nutrients they are receiving from sow's milk. Creep feed is formulated to maximise intake on the basis that the more food that a young pig eats the faster and more economically it will grow.

Piglets usually eat about 2 kg of creep feed in the period up to five weeks of age. Up to 21 days of age the larger pigs eat the most creep feed. As it is the milk that the piglet gets from the sow which causes him to be large, a high milk yield by the sow will encourage a high intake of creep by the piglet. After 21 days, pigs given a good start and of a reasonable weight, say 5·5 kg (12 lb), can maintain growth rate either on a combination of milk and creep (where milk is plentiful), or by increasing the consumption of creep in those circumstances where milk is limited. This response brings about the effect that piglets receiving a plentiful supply of milk after 21 days of age eat less creep feed, but those receiving less milk eat more creep. However, the smaller pigs at 21 days will be adversely affected at all times by a low yield of milk from the sow. Piglets of less than 4 kg

(9 lb) at three weeks of age are likely to have a low rate of creep feed consumption in any case, and this will not increase in response to a further reduction in milk intake.

Average rates of growth, together with the composition of growth, from birth to 20 kg are shown in Table 2.4. The table shows how the piglet rapidly increases both his rate of growth and fat in growth. Although at birth the pig contains only about 1 per cent of fat in the body, fat growth greatly outpaces protein growth in early life; so that by about 10 kg liveweight the ratio of protein to fat in the body has fallen to 1:1. Fat and protein formation then tend to keep pace with each other over the early growth phase from 10–30 kg. After 30 kg or so fat growth again outpaces protein deposition as has been shown in Figure 2.4.

At about the third week of life, the supply of nutrients from milk is inadequate to meet the requirements for growth in piglets. This ever-widening gap between nutrients in milk and nutrient need to maximise growth is bridged by intakes of solid food (Figure 2.8).

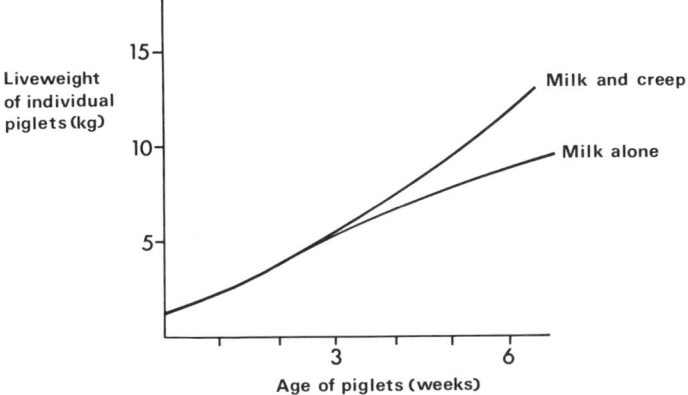

Figure 2.8. Growth of piglets with and without creep-feed.

LIFETIME PRODUCTION OF SOWS

Reductions in breeding regularity, fertility and longevity of sows may exceed the value to be gained from increasing short-term productivity by, for example, increasing litter size or frequency of farrowing.

The factors that cause problems in the breeding herd are difficult to identify but generally these conditions only appear in sows which are declining in weight or condition as lactation number increases.

Weight and body composition of sows

Most female pigs contain 30 per cent fat or more when they are mated for the first time, even although they are only 50 per cent of their mature body weight. As the sow gets older, according to the supplies of feed, she seeks to attain her target mature weight.

This attempt to attain her own target weight is made in the face of the considerable additional demands of pregnancy and lactation. Where feed is restricted, the sow reacts by breaking down her fat depots so that total fat in the body declines in each reproductive cycle.

It is not possible to define accurately the 'sticking point' at which the sow no longer readily draws on her fat reserves, but it is probably when she contains about 5–10 per cent fat. When this point is reached, it is usually accompanied by a reduction in fertility and failure to breed regularly. It is apparent that sow management must aim at selecting feeding regimes which specifically prevent this point being reached.

Under extreme conditions sows can become so emaciated that they react to stress by becoming subject to 'Thin Sow Syndrome'. The symptoms of this syndrome are a voracious appetite and an unprecedented loss of body weight. Only very high intakes of feed can arrest the process, although more usually the sow is a lost cause due to failure to breed or death.

Chapter 3

PROTEINS

PIGS ARE fed for the meat they produce. Where the dietary energy needs of mankind are all too readily supplied from vegetable sources, the principal rôle of meat must be as a concentrated protein source; but to provide protein-rich lean meat the pig must itself be fed proteins.

In the course of turning diet-protein into pigmeat protein, the animal concentrates the most useful elements of vegetable proteins into a form readily accepted for human consumption. The pig can be fed protein sources which are less willingly consumed by mankind than by pigs; for example, micro-organisms (SCP), offal, waste fish and by-products of the vegetable oil industry. Animal products, meat and bone meal, fish meal and so on, contain about 55–75 per cent protein; the oil seed residues such as extracted soya bean meal and ground nut meal contain 40–50 per cent protein; and field beans contain about 25 per cent protein. However, most protein eaten by pigs comes from cereals, which although only containing 8–12 per cent protein, usually comprise the major part of the pig's diet. Tables of the protein contents of feedstuffs are given at the end of the book in Appendix 2.

All conversion processes are inefficient to a certain degree and the conversion of pig-feed protein into meat is no exception. Protein is scarce, so the effort in pig nutrition is directed to minimising the financial penalties incurred through avoidable inefficiencies.

As a general rule, the proteins in meat and vegetables contain about 16 per cent nitrogen, so total protein content can be determined by multiplying nitrogen by the factor 6·25. Most studies of protein use by pigs have actually been studies of nitrogen use, and protein and nitrogen are often used as synonyms.

Proteins are made up of amino acids linked together into chains. When the proteins in feedstuffs are eaten, the special protease enzymes of the digestive system breaks them down into component amino acids or linked groups of amino acids. These smaller fractions are absorbed through the wall of the alimentary tract and into the blood stream, from whence they pass to the liver and around to the cells of the body. The greatest requirement for amino acids comes from the actively growing areas of the body and the mammary glands, particularly for the deposition of new protein in lean meat and milk. Protein is invariably laid down in the animal's body in association with water; lean meat is about three-quarters water and one-fifth protein. A 50 kg (110 lb) pig contains about 7·5 kg protein, 11 kg of fat, 1·5 kg mineral ash and 30 kg water. Sow's milk contains 6 per cent protein.

The mixture of amino acids which enters the blood from the alimentary tract is most unlikely to be in exactly the correct proportions that are needed by the body. But the liver has the ability of making new amino acids from those which are present in excess. In this way some of the differences between the supply from the feed and the needs of the animal can be adjusted. There are about ten amino acids which cannot be readily synthesised by the pig. These must be supplied in the diet, not only in the correct total quantity to satisfy the animal's needs, but also in the right proportion to each other; that is, correctly balanced. A commonly accepted list of these *essential* amino acids would be: lysine, methionine, cystine, threonine, phenylalanine, histidine, tryptophan, leucine, isoleucine, valine and arginine. Cystine can replace methionine to a certain extent and both contain sulphur; they are often combined together as methionine + cystine and termed the sulphur amino acids.

When the essential amino acids in the blood are not in the correct proportions for the body's needs, the excess are broken down and either synthesised into non-essential amino acids or excreted. There are three main routes by which the animal can excrete protein, or protein breakdown products, from within the body: in sweat, in intestinal secretions and, by far the most important, through the urine in the form of urea. When an amino acid is broken down to urea (deaminated), the nitrogen-containing fraction is separated from the carbon fraction releasing the carbon for use elsewhere in the body, for example in fat formation. Deamination does not therefore result in a total loss of utilisable elements of the protein molecule.

The remaining amino acids, correctly balanced, are linked together into the particular protein which the body requires. Being a complex procedure, and one which changes the existing order of things, linking together amino acids to make protein is energy-consuming. Indeed, one-third to one-half of the total energy expended by a growing pig may be used for purposes of driving the reactions involved in the synthesis of new lean tissues.

The formation of milk is similar to that of meat. The lactating sow differs from the growing animal in one important respect, however, her own body provides a source of protein for milk manufacture in addition to the protein which is digested from the alimentary tract. A sow absorbing insufficient protein to satisfy the needs for lactation may break down some of her own lean body tissues in order to provide amino acids for milk.

DIGESTIBILITY OF PROTEIN

The digestibility of a nutrient is the difference between the amount consumed and the amount excreted in the faeces. If 100 g of protein were eaten and 20 g of protein excreted in the faeces, then 80 g were digested and the digestibility would be 80 per cent. Table 3.1 shows that the digestibility values for protein differ amongst the various feedstuffs. The protein in most feedstuffs is between 75 and 90 per cent digestible. Some proteins are less digestible than others, however, and processing treatments can also drastically reduce digestibility. Protein in some feather meals, for example, may be only 25 per cent digestible. An average value for the digestibility of protein in a mixed pig diet containing conventional ingredients would be 80–85 per cent.

TABLE 3.1. Digestibility values (%) expected for some common feedstuffs

	Protein (nitrogen × 6·25)	Energy
Maize (ground)	85-90	85-90
Barley (ground)	80-85	75-85
Wheat (ground)	85-90	85-90
Wheat middlings	70-75	55-70
Extracted soya-bean meal	85-90	80-85
Dried fish meal	90-95	85-90

Metabolic faecal losses

In the course of digestion, copious quantities of enzymes are secreted into the alimentary tract. These are themselves protein in nature, and may not be completely re-absorbed back into the pig's body. In addition, mucosal cells from the intestine wall, also containing protein, are sloughed off into the tract as food passes down. These protein fractions join with the indigestible fraction of the diet protein and are voided in the faeces. Protein in faeces, but not of dietary origin, is termed metabolic faecal protein. The presence of these losses makes the digestibility of protein appear to be less than it truly is. The *true* digestibility is, however, of little practical interest, because as far as the pig is concerned, it is the net difference between intake and faecal losses which is important.

As animals grow bigger and eat more, metabolic losses increase, which causes digestibility to slightly decrease. Increasing the quantity of food eaten also increases the need for enzymes and the wear and tear on the gut lining. Usually, the more fibrous and abrasive the food the greater the associated metabolic faecal loss and the lower the digestibility of protein. The inclusion of straw, cereal husks or sand into pig diets is therefore likely to increase metabolic losses and reduce the digestible protein available to the pig. Wheat middlings have twice as much fibre as wheat meal; respective digestibilities are 70 and 85 per cent. Feeds with a low protein content and a high fibre content may therefore contribute little or no protein to the animal.

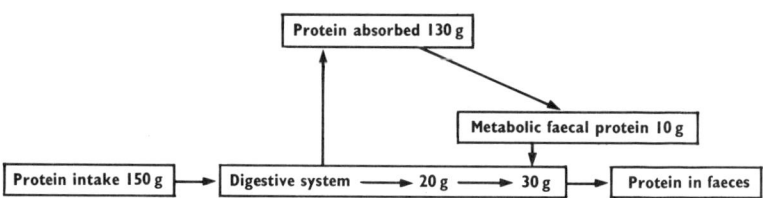

Losses of metabolic protein in the faeces amounts to 6–12 g for each kg of a concentrate feed containing in the region of 5 per cent fibre. For a pig consuming a diet with 150 g protein in each kg of feed metabolic faecal losses amount to about 30 per cent of total protein in faeces.

Particle size and structure

When the protein is contained within large particles, very coarsely ground grain for example, the protein digesting enzymes may not penetrate the whole piece of material before the food has passed down the tract, with the consequence that digestibility is reduced. Pigs do not digest well the complex structural cellulose, hemi-cellulose and lignin compounds which make up the cell walls, fibres and strengthening support frames of plants. Nitrogen may be present in structural compounds themselves, or contained in cell constituents surrounded by these structural compounds. Where the feed has not been pulverised and cells remain intact, the protein will pass through the animal poorly digested.

Enzymes also need *time* to work on the feed. An increase in the rate of passage of feed through the alimentary tract has the same effect as the protein being contained within a large particle of feed or surrounded by poorly digestible cell structures. If digestion is not completed before the feed passes beyond the small intestine, digestibility will be reduced.

Heat damage

Feedstuffs are heated to dry them to facilitate handling and storage, or heating may be a part of some manufacturing process imposed upon the material. Heating alters the structure of proteins and makes them less useful as nutrient sources. Classical cases of heat damage have been in soya-bean meals, meat and blood meals, and fish meals. The greater the degree of heating the less digestible the protein. All heating will reduce digestibility of protein to a certain extent, but the effects of controlled cooking, micronisation and drying are generally quite small (about 5 per cent). When the heat treatment is improperly controlled, the digestibility may be reduced very markedly, digestibility of less than 50 per cent not being exceptional for a heat damaged protein source. Where a protein source has been subjected to a process which might bring about protein damage, it would therefore be unwise to reach conclusions about its value on the basis of an analysis for protein (nitrogen) content alone.

The digestibility, or 'availability', of the amino acid lysine is often a good indicator of the extent of heat damage. When a protein is overheated, lysine may become 'bound' to other chemical compounds and thus be made unavailable. There is a chemical test for determining the proportion of total lysine which is 'available lysine', and this can be a useful measure of protein quality in a feed.

Inhibitors

Many plant materials contain organic compounds, themselves protein in nature, which inhibit the action of the protease enzymes and so reduce protein digestibility. Protease inhibitors act in a general way in the gut and their effect is not restricted to the feedstuff which contains them. The inclusion into a diet of a feed with inhibitor activity reduces the digestibility of all the protein in the diet.

Field beans contain sufficient protease inhibitor activity measurably to reduce the efficiency of utilisation of protein from this potentially important pig feed. Raw potatoes contain very powerful protease inhibitors. Perhaps the most familiar feed containing protease inhibitor activity is the soya bean; *raw* soya-bean protein is poorly digested as a result.

Like other proteins, protease inhibitors are changed upon heating, and in the course of this change they lose their active properties. So after oil extraction, the soya-bean meal imported into Britain from the USA is toasted.

METABOLISM OF DIGESTED PROTEIN

The active protein fractions absorbed into the pig's body are: (1) essential amino acids, which must be absorbed *as such* and cannot be synthesised by the body, (2) non-essential amino acids, (3) other non-protein nitrogen containing compounds, some of which can be used to make non-essential amino acids. The various protein fractions are put to the task of maintaining body tissues, and making muscle, connective tissues, body enzymes and the like.

Protein recycling

Protein in the body is not stable. Rather, the whole protein mass of the body is constantly recycled; that is, broken down and renewed. No process being completely efficient, there is wastage during each cycle of breakdown and renewal. The waste products of this cycle join the pool of amino acids formed from over-supply or imbalance. From here they are either re-synthesised to make new protein or are broken down further and the nitrogen is excreted as waste urea. The losses of protein from the recycling process must be made good if the lean mass is to be maintained.

It is reasonable to assume that the protein fractions resulting from the breakdown of existing body protein are ideal in amino acid balance for building up new body protein. The percentage efficiency with which protein is recycled is therefore likely to be high, but the loss of protein also depends upon the mass of body protein involved in recycling. Thus the larger the lean mass of the pig the greater will be the losses. Another factor affecting losses of protein resultant from the cycling of body tissues, is the rate at which the cycle takes place. The faster protein is broken down and built up the greater will be the daily loss. Protein recycling is fastest in young, rapidly growing pigs.

Balance of essential amino acids

Quality, in the nutritional sense, is taken as the balance of digested essential amino acids. To accord to a protein feed its true value per unit of protein it is necessary: (a) to define the amino acid balance needed by the pig for purposes of maintenance, growth and milk production, and (b) to compare the amino acid balance in the feed with that needed by the pig. Crop plants do not manufacture proteins of the ideal amino acid spectrum for pig use; some inefficiency is therefore unavoidable.

The perfect balance of essential amino acids is the one which meets all the various needs of the body for amino acids. Some guide to the amino acid needs of a growing pig may be found in the amino acid compostion of pigmeat shown in Table 3.2 compared with the amino acid composition of four feedstuff proteins. It is noticeable from Table 3.2 that barley appears to be deficient in lysine, a deficiency not shared by the other proteins. If the balance of absorbed amino acids is not perfect in relation to the animal's needs, the pig will adjust back to the amino acid which is in shortest supply—the 'first-limiting' amino acid; or, in the case of barley, lysine.

TABLE 3.2. Some amino acids (%) in the protein of pig meat and some feedstuffs

	Meat protein	*Barley protein*	*Ex. soya-bean protein*	*Fish meal protein*	*A microbial protein*
Lysine	7·0	3·8	6·6	6·6	6·3
Methionine + cystine	2·7	2·3	2·8	3·7	3·0
Threonine	3·5	3·0	4·2	4·5	4·6
Tryptophan	0·8	1·6	1·3	1·4	1·0

The body functions requiring amino acids, for example muscle growth, may be likened to a water tub. This analogy is shown in Figure 3.1–6. The number of staves (amino acids) in the tub is fixed, as is the proportionality of their widths. But the height of the staves or size of the tub is not fixed. In Figure 3.2 the diet supply of tryptophan and threonine is sufficient for a tub the same size as shown in Figure 3.1, but the lysine supply is sufficient to make only a smaller tub. It is axiomatic that to make a larger tub all that is needed is more lysine, then no threonine and less tryptophan would go to waste. The height of the tub, or rate of muscle protein growth which it represents, can accordingly be increased by the supplementation of the first limiting amino acid (lysine). In the case shown, there is no need to increase total protein supply, merely to improve the amino acid balance.

The barrel analogy also shows how two proteins with different amino acid balances can supplement each other. The protein described by the staves in Figure 3.4 is as imbalanced as was that shown in Figure 3.2; fed alone, this would only make a low tub. However, if both proteins (3.2 and 3.4) were fed together they would complement each other, such that two small tubs do not just make their sum (about half a barrel) but a whole barrel (Figure 3.5).

In cereals, lysine is usually the first-limiting amino acid. Fish products are particularly high in lysine, as is soya-bean meal. These two protein sources therefore complement cereals well.

With high quality proteins it is possible to achieve an efficiency of retention of digested protein as high as 70 per cent. The fact that for most conventional pig feeds something like 50 per cent of the digested protein will be lost is sufficient to indicate that amino acid imbalance

46 PRACTICAL PIG NUTRITION

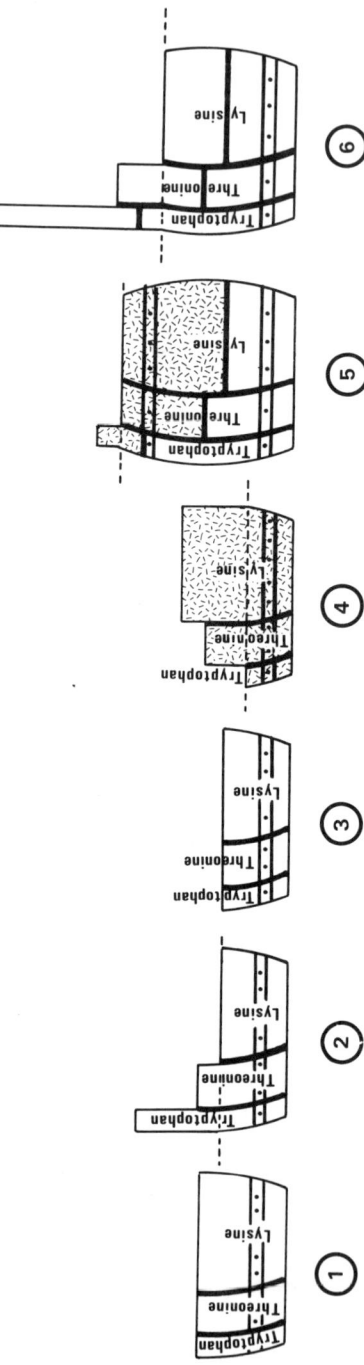

Figure 3. 1-6. The barrel analogy for amino acid balance.

is a major cause of inefficiency in protein utilisation. This is not to say that the feeding of imbalanced protein is not feasible. Imbalanced protein sources, or combinations of protein sources which remain imbalanced, are usually much cheaper than more nearly perfectly balanced proteins. It is often economically advantageous to feed more of a lower quality protein and to accept a higher rate of wastage. The shortage of lysine in Figure 3.2 could be alleviated simply by feeding the animal more of the protein. This situation is shown in Figure 3.6. Productive capacity of the animal has been doubled, but the penalty in terms of lost amino acids has to be paid.

Sometimes, the cheaper protein sources are found as a minor component of vegetable feedstuffs in combination with starch or oil. If this method of supplying protein is used, the animal may be inundated with too much energy. For example, it is quite possible to provide the total amino acid needs for a growing pig by feeding barley alone. However, in doing this the animal would have to eat so much barley energy that it would become too fat. The greater the animal's needs for protein, the more reliance must be placed upon the concentrated sources of better quality proteins, such as fish meal and soya.

Amino acid supplementation with synthetic amino acids

Where one amino acid is in short supply and is the first limiting, it follows that supplementation with that amino acid will produce a marked improvement in the amino acid balance. This, in turn, will increase the efficiency of utilisation and reduce protein losses via the urine. The beneficial nature of the response may be out of all proportion to the small addition made of a single amino acid. Growth response which results from amino acid supplementation is *not* a response to that amino acid *per se,* but a response to an improved supply of all the essential amino acids brought about by the balancing abilities of the supplement.

Usually, in diets based on cereals, lysine is first limiting, with methionine + cystine or threonine next. In diets based on maize, tryptophan can be limiting. Often when a lysine limitation is remedied, methionine + cystine or threonine will become limiting, and so it is possible to supplement with one amino acid after the other until the protien supply is correctly balanced.

Unfortunately, most synthetic amino acids are expensive. In many cases provision of animal protein, even with all but the needed amino acid going to waste, can be cheaper than the manufacture of a single amino acid. The probable exceptions are methionine and lysine. Synthetic lysine can be produced by fermentation at a price which is often competitive with lysine in fish meal. Responses to synthetic lysine are the same as to natural lysine at the lower levels of addition, although at higher levels, response seems to tail off much earlier. Synthetic lysine is most appropriate to correct a small imbalance rather than a large one. The manufacture of synthetic D–L methionine from acrolein is comparatively cheap.

In the short term, only lysine, and possibly methionine, tryptophan and threonine, are likely to be considered as amino acid supplements. Shortages of other amino acids, and more often than not of those named, are likely to be met by total protein supplementation rather than specific amino acid supplementation. The decision to use a natural protein rather than a synthetic amino acid is economic, and depends upon their comparative prices per unit of response obtained.

Responses to synthetic amino acid additions tend to be variable. One reason for this may be that the selection of a single amino acid for a supplement assumes perfect knowledge that the amino acid in question was the first limiting to the exact extent of the level of the supplementation—a degree of precision rarely obtained. Supplementation by use of a natural protein may be more expensive, but may also correct other amino acid imbalances.

Non-essential amino acid nitrogen and non-protein nitrogen (NPN)

Protein nitrogen is also absorbed into the body in the form of amino acids which are not in the essential group, and there is a fraction of non-amino nitrogen-containing compounds. There are also available in the body the waste amino acids resultant from imbalance of feed protein in relation to the needs of the pig. All these nitrogen sources join a pool of non-essential nitrogen in the body.

The pig has the ability to change some of these fractions and to make from them whatever the current non-essential amino acid needs might be. In the barrel analogy (Figure 3.1–6), the completed barrel is made up of staves representing both essential and non-essential amino acids in about equal proportions. Only the essential ones must be supplied in the diet, the others the body can make for itself. The efficiency with which the non-essential pool is used will depend upon the respective proportions of essential to non-essential amino acids needed by the tissue undergoing synthesis.

To have essential amino acids in abundance, but not other nitrogen sources, would merely cause the breakdown of essential amino acids to create the non-essential ones. Alternatively, to have a feed source which provided excess of non-essential protein nitrogen would not increase the rate of synthesis of a protein tissue in the pig above the limit set by the first limiting essential amino acid.

The remaining fraction of dietary nitrogen is the non-protein nitrogen (NPN) part which is made from compounds which contain nitrogen but which are neither protein nor amino acid. Examples would be the nucleic acids of micro-organisms, and urea and ammonium salts fed as NPN sources to cattle. The ruminant can make good use of NPN because the microbes of the rumen convert it to microbial protein. The pig, being monogastric, has no such facility, so the NPN just adds to the animal's waste nitrogen pool. If the diet is deficient in total protein, but there are ample essential amino acids, then some of the NPN could be used for the synthesis of non-essential amino acids. In normal pig diets this is not usually the case. There is no deficiency of non-essential amino acid nitrogen, so non-protein nitrogen is only very poorly used by pigs, if at all. The possible exception would be where the microflora of the pig's caecum and large intestine could work like the microbes of the rumen and synthesise microbial protein from NPN.

Dietary supply of amino acids

Individual amino acids are relevant only in the context of total amino acid supply. Dietary needs are best defined by a statement of the required protein quality in terms of essential amino acid balance, together with the total protein need. Total protein need will vary with rate of growth but the essential amino acid balance will not vary greatly. Some guide to the appropriate essential amino acid content of protein in pig diets is given in Table 3.3. The amino acid content of the *diet itself* will depend upon the concentration of the protein included in the diet.

Time-base for protein synthesis

Protein needs for protein maintenance are fixed for any one period of time, although they vary with the physiological state of the animal.

TABLE 3.3. Guide to amino acid composition of protein appropriate to the diets of growing pigs, pregnant sows, and lactating sows

Amino acid	Percentage of the protein		
	Growing pigs	Pregnant sows	Lactating sows
Lysine	5·5	3·5	3·8
Threonine	3·2	2·8	2·6
Methionine + cystine	3·1	2·5	2·5
Tryptophan	1·0	0·8	0·8
Histidine	1·5	2·1	1·9
Leucine	5·0	7·6	6·4
Isoleucine	3·5	3·7	4·5
Valine	3·5	4·4	4·6
Tyrosine + phenylalanine	3·5	6·3	6·3

Similarly, there appears to be a limit to the amount of new protein tissue that the pig can synthesise in any given period (see Table 2.3). If this time period is assumed to be 24 hours, then a daily supply of dietary protein less than that which the animal could use would result in a failure to realise the full potential for synthesis of new protein. Conversely, an over-supply of dietary protein will result in the *pro rata* urinary excretion of the excess.

The ability of an animal to compensate for vagaries of protein supply is crucial to the protein economy of the pig; and knowledge of the time-base involved for protein deposition is critical to pig feeding strategy. At present this aspect of protein metabolism is controversial. If a pig fails to grow protein at the maximum rate on one day because insufficient protein is supplied, then if this insufficiency is made good the next day by provision of extra protein, can protein growth proceed at greater than the maximum rate? Or, once lost, is that day's protein synthesis gone forever? What is the time limit within which compensation could take place—a day? a week? a month?

For the present, as the evidence for compensatory protein growth is not substantial, it is assumed that the time limit for compensation is only one day; and potential protein growth, once lost, is irretrievable.

There is, of course, no problem about compensatory protein growth if there is no necessity for the pig to grow protein at the maximum possible rate. An average daily rate of protein growth less than the maximum can be attained by compensation within the ceiling limit to the daily rate. It is only when compensation requires the limit to be exceeded that doubt arises about the realities of compensatory growth.

Biological value (BV)

Biological value is a single numerical value ascribed to a protein which gives an estimate of the relationship between the essential amino acid balance of the diet protein and the essential amino acid needs of the pig. The principle of biological value for proteins has been described in Figure 3.1-6.

If the biological value of a protein is 70, then for each 100 g of protein absorbed, 30 g is judged not to be useful on account of amino acid imbalances. The remaining 70 g is available for protein metabolism; some will be used in the processes of protein recycling and some will be retained in the body as protein growth or synthesised into milk protein.

The protein in fish has a biological value of about 77. Most cereal proteins are deficient in one or other of the essential amino acids and their BV is often around 50. Soya bean protein is of similar value to fish protein. Biological values for a range of feed ingredients are given in Appendix 2. The BV of the protein in conventional mixed pig diets is usually about 60 to 70.

PROTEIN REQUIREMENTS OF GROWING PIGS

Although the calculation of protein requirement is complicated by protein recycling, an approximation can still be made.

Protein is needed first to replace recycling losses (maintenance). About 15 per cent of the live weight is protein, and 13·6 per cent of this is recycled daily; the amount decreasing as the pig grows. The fractional losses from recycling are about 0·06. So, to estimate 'maintenance' requirement, live weight can be multiplied by a factor which decreases from about 0·0012 (0·15 × 0·13 × 0·06 = 0·0012) at 20 kg, to 0·0005 (0·15 × 0·06 × 0·06 = 0·0005) at 120 kg.

The amount of protein required in the diet further depends upon the biological value of the protein and upon the amount digested (the digestibility coefficient).

EXAMPLE 1:

A growing pig of 50 kg needs 0·0009 × 50 kg = 45 g protein for 'maintenance'. If the pig grows 450 g of lean, 22 per cent of 450 g = 100 g protein. The requirement is for 100 + 45 = 145 g protein.

If the biological value of the diet protein is 65 then the digested protein required is 145/0·65 = 223 g digested protein. If the digestibility of the diet protein is 80 per cent, then 223/0·8 = 280 g daily of dietary protein.

EXAMPLE 2:

To grow the same amount of lean on the same diet as the pig in example 1, an 80 kg pig would need: 0·0007 × 80 kg = 56 g + 100 g = 156 g protein/(0·65 × 0·8) = 300 g daily of dietary protein.

Pigs would require proportionately more of a protein with a lower biological value and/or a lower digestibility.

EXAMPLE 3:

If a 40 kg pig was fed 1·75 kg of a diet which contained 14 per cent of dietary protein with a biological value of 65 and a digestibility of 80 per cent, then it may be calculated that if lean growth contains about 22 per cent protein, the pig could grow 395 g of lean daily.
1·75 × 0·14 × 0·65 × 0·8 = 127 g protein available
0·001 × 40 = 40 g protein for maintenance
127 − 40 = 87 g protein/0·22 = 395 g lean.

PROTEIN METABOLISM IN THE PREGNANT SOW

In the pregnant sow, protein goes to the products of conception; foetuses and membranes. More protein is needed to maintain losses resultant from protein cycling, and to build up mammary tissue ready for the lactation which will ensue. In addition, protein may be used to lay up protein stores in the maternal body; stores which would then be available to support lactation in the event of a dietary protein shortage at that time. This mechanism is a useful natural adaptation; but where an adequate protein supply is expected in the lactation diet, failure to create depot stores of protein will not result in any protein shortage in the piglet's milk supply.

Lastly, the sow has the capacity to reach her mature lean mass by the fourth litter or so; the potential for continued protein deposition in the maternal body of the sow is therefore considerable. If protein growth is to be encouraged in addition to the reproductive functions of sows, the requisite dietary allowances must be made.

These various requirements are not easily distinguished from one another. There is no reason to believe that the sow makes any arbitrary division of her reproductive processes. It is likely, for example, that the demands of lactation are prepared for as soon as it becomes apparent that there will be a lactation, that is, at the *conception* of the litter which will suckle, not at its birth.

Most of the growth of conception products occurs between day 80 of pregnancy and term at 114 days. About 3 g of protein are deposited daily in the uterus at day 15 of the pregnancy, 10 g at day 50, 20 g at day 75, and 50 g at day 114. Protein deposition in the mammary gland is much less, and only reaches a maximum of 10 g protein daily just prior to parturition. Total growth achieved as a direct result of pregnancy amounts to about 10–12 kg of piglets, 2·5 kg membranes, 3 kg of uterine growth and about 2 kg of mammary tissues. This is 18 kg or more of gain, most of which is protein and water. If these tissues are about 12 per cent protein, then the total protein gain is 2·2 kg. Averaged over the last 34 days of pregnancy, this amounts to 65 g protein daily.

Cycling of the protein mass proceeds at an ever slower rate as the animal ages and it may be speculated that it reaches a value of about 5 per cent of the protein mass daily when the animal is mature.

The efficiency of use of protein for purposes of synthesis of body protein is, of course, largely dependent upon the biological value of the dietary protein ingested. Biological value depends upon the needs of the animal and the efficiency with which the animal can convert the dietary protein; as well as being a function of the diet protein source itself. Thus it has been observed that pregnant sows, particularly towards the end of their pregnancy, appear to utilise protein more efficiently than the non-pregnant. This phenomenon, usually referred to as pregnancy anabolism, results from the metabolic and hormonal changes associated with pregnancy.

PROTEIN REQUIREMENTS OF PREGNANT SOWS

Lack of adequate data jeopardise calculations of this nature, but nevertheless a logical examination of the protein needs of the pregnant sow can be attempted.

Pregnant sows given diets with no protein, lose in the urine 5–6 g nitrogen daily. This is equivalent to 35 g protein. The calculated value from protein recycling is rather higher at 50–60 g protein.

Daily lean gain made by sows in pregnancy is directly under the control of the feeder. Sows may readily make maternal weight gains of 5–50 kg in pregnancy. If the normal allowance of about 20 kg of maternal live gain is allowed in pregnancy, this will contain about 3 kg of protein; equivalent to 26 g daily.

The requirements of pregnancy itself have been calculated to be small in the first half of pregnancy, but about 65 g daily in the last 30 days or so. Taking 60 g as the maintenance requirement, the need is for about 86 g daily (60 + 26) in the first 80 days and about 151 g daily (86 + 65) in the last 30 days. If the biological value of the dietary protein for the first part of pregnancy is 60, and the digestibility is 80 per cent, then the requirement is for 143 g digested protein or 179 g dietary protein daily. If a higher biological value of 80 is allowed in the later stages of pregnancy, due to increased efficiency of protein use by the pregnant animal, then the daily requirement over the last 30 days is 189 g digested protein or 236 g dietary protein. Because of the improvement in the efficiency of protein use by pregnant sows in the later stages of pregnancy, the daily requirement does not change greatly over the whole of pregnancy, and averages 170 g of digestible protein or 210 g of dietary protein daily. The quality of the protein in pregnant sow diets should be similar to that of growing pigs. The suggested balance of amino acids in the protein is given in Table 3.3. Should the protein quality of the diet be lower than this, the amount of digested protein required in the diet should be raised accordingly.

Protein growth in the sow herself comprises only 20–30 per cent or so of the protein requirements. As this is the only aspect of protein use by pregnant sows which is freely controllable, there is much less flexibility allowed in the protein provision to pregnant sows than, for example, to growing pigs.

PROTEIN METABOLISM IN THE LACTATING SOW

Sow's milk contains 6 per cent protein. With a daily output of milk of 5 to 7 kg (depending upon litter size), the daily secretion of milk protein is 300–420 g. Protein secretion in milk is akin to protein deposition in the muscle of a young rapidly growing animal. The mammary tissue is small in mass compared to the amount of protein it synthesises; it is extremely active metabolically and the tissue of the gland is recycled very rapidly. Quantitative information on these aspects of protein metabolism is scarce, but it appears that the efficiency with which the gland uses blood amino acids for milk protein synthesis is at least 65 per cent (compared with 30–50 per cent for muscle synthesis).

For the first 4–5 days of the lactation the sow experiences a flush of nitrogen in milk and urine. This probably relates to some readjustment of metabolism following parturition. Losses are greater for animals which have had a more generous protein allowance in pregnancy. This phenomenon upsets estimates of protein requirements in early lactation, but is of sufficiently short duration to have an insignificant effect upon protein nutrition as a whole.

Milk protein production is buffered to a certain extent against the vagaries of dietary protein supply. Changes in diet protein intake do not bring about immediate concomitant changes in milk protein secretion. To synthesise milk protein, the mammary tissue draws upon the pool of blood amino acids. This pool is supplied both by dietary and internal sources. Thus, if the dietary supply of protein is withheld, the sow will break down some of her own body protein to supply the needs of the suckling young. This ability of the sow to draw on body reserves of protein is, however, limited, and severe shortages of dietary protein, or a deficiency over a long period of time cannot be made good. In these cases, protein secreted in the milk diminishes. Under normal dietary conditions, losses of body lean from the sow are generally to be avoided; or if incurred, soon replenished.

PROTEIN REQUIREMENTS OF LACTATING SOWS

Protein requirements of lactating sows are very largely a function of the amount of milk she is giving. This in turn is dependent upon the number of young suckling and the stage of lactation. Minor manipulations of the protein supply to lactating sows will not bring about any marked changes in milk production or piglet growth. There will, however, be a change in the body composition of the sow.

A sow yielding 7 kg of milk daily produces 420 g protein in the milk. An efficiency of conversion of 70 per cent leads to a requirement for digested protein of 600 g. To this should be added the maintenance requirement already approximated to be about 60 g net, or 86 g of digested protein. If the sow is maintained with a slight positive gain, of say 50 g daily, requiring a further 70 g or so of digested protein then the total requirement for digested protein would be 756 g daily (600 + 86 + 70). With a digestibility coefficient of 0·8 this amounts to 945 g of dietary protein daily. A sow yielding 5 kg of milk daily would require correspondingly less protein and the requirement would be about 730 g dietary protein daily.

A severe reduction in total dietary protein supplied to the sow leads to a reduction in milk yield. The effect of protein intakes of below about 650 g will therefore be lowered milk production as well as an increased rate of breakdown of protein in the body of the sow. Whilst the sow can use her own body proteins to buffer short-term shortages in dietary protein supply, she cannot 'milk off her back' with respect to protein in the same way, as is possible with body stores of fat.

The dietary requirement will, of course, also depend upon the biological value of protein and the digestibility of the dietary protein source, which may well be more or less than the 80 per cent value used for these examples.

Chapter 4

ENERGY

ENERGY IS the most important feed constituent, costing more in total than any other dietary element. Most of the energy fed to animals is wasted, in as much as it is not to be found in the saleable products which leave the pig unit. Part of the energy losses are unavoidable, but a further part relate to inefficiencies of energy use which can be controlled.

The body needs energy first as a power source for metabolism. Metabolic processes include maintaining life support systems such as heart activity, lung and body muscle activity, renewal of worn-out cells and the recycling of existing body tissue. Energy is also needed to synthesise the new tissues of growth, pregnancy and lactation: protein, fat and lactose. In addition, energy is contained *within* the stored and secreted products. Energy is also required to maintain body temperature in cold environments.

Energy is yielded by the oxidation of carbohydrates, fats or proteins. The glucose units of carbohydrate and the fatty acids of fats are the most appropriate for purposes of producing energy for metabolism. Glucose can also be used for forming the carbon elements of non-essential amino acids, for fatty acid synthesis and for lactose formation. Fat is very high in energy, and it may be used in the pig for yielding energy or for the direct re-synthesis of body fat. Protein is the least efficiently used of all sources of energy, not only is it a scarce resource and needed in the synthesis of new body protein, but before a protein can yield energy, it must be broken down to urea (deaminated), which consumes energy.

Carbohydrates are built from compounds like glucose and cellulose. These compounds are linked up into ever more complex structures. The best known of the plant carbohydrates are starch and fibre. Starch is readily broken down by digestive amylase enzymes into fractions which are small enough to be absorbed. In contrast, most of the fibrous structures of plants are complex celluloses, hemi-celluloses and lignins. By their very complexity, these structural compounds are difficult for the digestive system of the pig to deal with. Further, the pig does not have enzymes specific for digesting

ENERGY

cellulose. As a generalisation, it can be assumed that these structural carbohydrates, usually referred to simply as the fibre fraction, are more likely to be indigestible than digestible.

Fats are acted upon in the digestive tract by bile salts and by lipases, they are absorbed into the body as their component fatty acids and glycerides, and also as small integral fat particles (triglyceride). Soft fats, such as coconut oil, appear to be better digested than hard fats such as beef tallow. A part of the dietary fat may often appear in the pig's body fat unchanged, a further fraction may have required only a little alteration for it to be a suitable component of pig fat, and another fraction may have undergone complete breakdown and resynthesis before being deposited in the body.

In Table 4.1 is shown the energy yield from 1 kilo of a conventional pig diet. The unit of measurement for energy is the mega joule, abbreviated MJ. It can be seen that while most of the energy comes from starch which has 17·4 MJ energy/kg, the protein fraction of the diet also contains a significant quantity of dietary energy, 23·6 MJ/kg. With 39·3 MJ/kg, the presence of fat enhances the energy content of the diet. Fibre, because it is so poorly digestible decreases the energy value of diets.

TABLE 4.1. **Energy yield from the components of one kilogram dry matter of a conventional diet**

	Energy content (MJ/kg)	Approximate digestibility (%)	Proportion of diet dry matter (%)	Energy yield (MJ of digested energy)	Energy yield (% of total digested energy)
Carbohydrates					
—starchy	17·4	90	65	10·1	66·0
—fibrous	17·4	10	6	0·1	0·6
Proteins	23·6	85	19	3·8	25·0
Fats	39·3	70	5	1·4	9·0

In Table 4.2 is given an energy balance for a 50 kg pig eating daily 2 kg of feed and having available for body metabolism about 26 MJ of energy. Thirty-five per cent of the energy is used for purposes of maintaining the animal, and 25 per cent for driving the metabolic processes associated with the growth of protein and fat. In total, 60 per cent of the energy leaves the animal's body as heat and is lost by dissipation into the environment. The remaining 40 per cent is retained in the tissues of growth. Most of the energy in growth is contained in fat. Fat comprises two-thirds of new growth, and contains over three-quarters of the energy in new growth.

Pig growth contains water in addition to protein and fat. Most of this water is associated with protein, the two together making lean meat. In the example pig in Table 4.2 lean growth would be about 450 g and fat growth about 220 g. In terms of liveweight growth there is 2·4 MJ energy in 450 g lean and 7·9 MJ in 220 g fat, or about 5 MJ/kg lean and 36 MJ/kg fat. After adding on the energy used to drive the chemical reactions involved in the synthesis of new protein and fat, the total energy cost of lean tissue growth is about 14 MJ/kg of lean and the energy cost of fat growth is about 49 MJ/kg.

TABLE 4.2. An energy balance for a 50 kg pig

	MJ of energy	% of total
Used up in metabolism and lost as heat:		
Maintenance of existing state	9·0	35
Driving protein synthesis	3·6	14
Driving fat synthesis	2·8	11
Deposited in the tissues of pig growth:		
In protein (100 g)	2·4	9
In fat (200 g)	7·9	31

Energetically, fat growth is therefore about $3\frac{1}{2}$ times more costly than lean growth. But fat growth is not the most costly energetic process, the prize for this goes to maintenance. In the example, maintenance costs more than any other energy function, 35 per cent of total energy supply—and this in a rapidly growing animal. The slower the growth, the higher will be the proportion of total energy spent on maintenance, and all the maintenance energy is lost as heat. Fat growth is more efficient than slow growth or no growth.

DIGESTIBILITY OF ENERGY

A comparison of the composition of the feed eaten and the faeces excreted after digestion shows that the least digestible fractions are fibre and minerals (Table 4.3).

Energy in protein follows the same absorption and excretion patterns of the protein in which it is contained. The digestibility of dietary fats and oils by pigs appears to vary from 20–90 per cent. For fat contained in conventional cereal and animal products, and also for vegetable and animal fat added to pig diets as an additional energy source, a digestibility value of 70–80 per cent seems a reasonable expectation.

The digestibility of carbohydrates in the form of starch is high; about 95 per cent. However, the presence of structural carbohydrate compounds—fibre—in a feed reduces the overall digestibility of dietary energy. Indeed, the quantity of plant fibre in the diet is the major determinant of energy digestibility in naturally occurring diet ingredients. The complex cellulose compounds are themselves resistant to enzyme attack and the presence of indigestible material protects other dietary carbohydrates, proteins and lipids. In this way potentially digestible material can pass through the intestine unscathed. The protection afforded by structural plant compounds is related to the size of the fragments of plant material when they reach the digestive system. Thus, barley starch will be better digested if it is presented in a ground form, rather than surrounded by the structural elements of a whole barley grain.

TABLE 4.3. Approximate composition of feed and faeces

	Feed	Faeces
Dry matter weight (kg)	2	0·36
Percentage composition of the dry matter:		
Carbohydrates	70	40
Fat	5	8
Protein	15	13
Fibre	5	25
Ash	5	14

There is evidence that pigs, particularly when they are mature, do have a limited capability for digesting cellulose with the bacterial flora of the large intestine and caecum. It is generally assumed that the abilities of the pig in this direction are particularly limited, and indeed on conventional diets the pig has little need for an active cellulose-degrading bacterial flora. However, where low-density/high-fibre diets (such as wheatfeeds and grass meals) are concerned, more knowledge of the capability of the pig to deal with cellulose compounds is of considerable importance.

Figure 4.1 shows the improvement in digestibility with reduction in the particle size of cereal grains. It can be seen that the improvement is marked as soon as the integrity of the grain is destroyed by coarse grinding; the improvement from coarse grinding to fine grinding is much more slight. In Figure 4.2 is shown the effect of fibre in the diet ingredients. The fall in digestibility is quite rapid. Cooked potato with 2 per cent fibre may be 96 per cent digestible, but barley with about 5 per cent fibre is unlikely to be more than 85 per cent digestible; a wheat-feed with about 12 per cent fibre has a digestibility around 50 per cent.

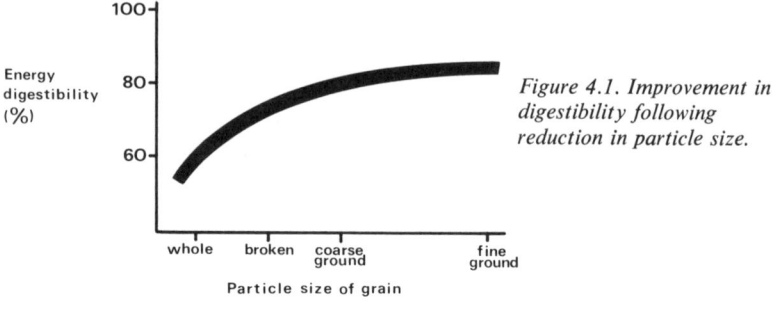

Figure 4.1. Improvement in digestibility following reduction in particle size.

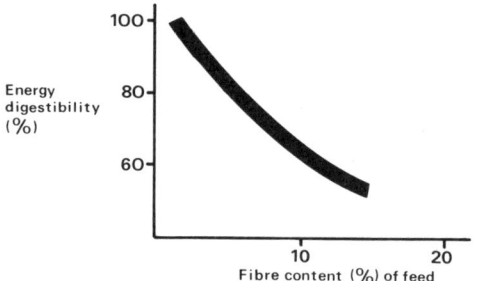

Figure 4.2. Reduction in digestibility with increasing fibrousness of diet ingredients.

METABOLISM OF DIGESTED ENERGY

Digestible energy (abbreviated DE) less the small losses of energy in the urine, is referred to as the metabolisable energy or ME. In the pig there are some further losses of energy in gasses leaving the body as belches and anal escapes, but generally these are small enough to be ignored. It is the ME which is the energy available for body metabolism and productive processes. The urine of growing pigs contains about 0·04–0·05 MJ/g nitrogen. When urinary losses of nitrogen increase due to over-consumption of protein, or to amino acid imbalance, the ME becomes a lower proportion of the DE. With an all-barley diet of 11 per cent crude protein, ME is about 97 per cent of DE, whereas for a diet containing fishmeal with 25 per cent crude protein, ME is 94 per cent of DE.

Maintenance

Maintenance needs relate to the size of the animal but there are economies of scale, smaller animals having higher maintenance requirements in relation to their body weight. For purposes of calculating the energetic expenditure of maintenance, this economy of scale is allowed for by raising the normal body weight of the animal to the power 0·75. Liveweight$^{0.75}$ or 'metabolic' body weight is given in Appendix 1.

Estimates of maintenance needs of pigs vary between 0·4 and 0·5 MJ ME/kg metabolic body weight. When considering the efficiency of production of liveweight gain, foetuses or milk, the energy costs of maintenance are a loading for which there is no output. A pig receiving just enough ME for maintenance is infinitely inefficient; it consumes food but produces nothing. For any given level of energy intake a larger pig is less efficient in terms of food used/liveweight gained than a smaller one, since its total maintenance needs are greater. Table 4.4 typifies the situation for growing pigs.

TABLE 4.4. Efficiencies of pigs of different bodyweights

	Body weight of pig (kg)		
	25	50	100
Same amount of energy intake:			
Intake of energy from 1·5 kg of diet (MJ ME)	18	18	18
Needs for maintenance (MJ ME)	5·3	8·9	15·0
Available for growth (MJ ME)	12·7	9·1	3·0
Energy eaten/energy stored	2·6	3·6	11·0
Daily live-weight gain (kg)	0·66	0·48	0·16
Food used/live weight gained	2·3	3·1	9·4
Same amount of growth:			
Daily live weight gained (kg)	0·7	0·7	0·7
Needs for maintenance (MJ ME)	5·3	8·9	15·0
Needs for growth (MJ ME)	15·7	15·7	15·7
Food needed (kg)	1·8	2·1	2·6
Food used/live weight gained	2·6	3·0	3·7

Production

The energy cost of protein growth has been estimated at about 69 MJ/kg protein. If protein itself contains 24 MJ of energy, then about 45 MJ are used to drive the synthetic processes and are ultimately lost as heat; the efficiency of energy use for the deposition of new protein is about 35 per cent. To convert absorbed fat into body fat appears to be relatively more simple and often the final product (pig fat) bears a resemblance to the dietary fat. The efficiency with which energy is used for fat deposition is about 75 per cent. With fat in the body containing 39 MJ of energy, the total energy cost of fat deposition appears to be around 54 MJ/kg fat. In addition to the energy used for maintenance, therefore, each kg of new protein synthesised uses up about 45 MJ of energy and each kg of new fat formed uses up about 14 MJ of energy; all of this energy goes to waste as heat losses.

Figure 4.3 shows the energy balance of pigs as they grow from 20 to 120 kilo. As the pig grows, energy used for maintenance increases with the size of the animal. In the initial stages of growth, protein deposition may increase and the energy in protein increases accordingly. After about 40 kilo, in the example, the quantity of energy going daily into new body protein remains fairly stable. Conversely, the energy which is held daily in new fat increases as the pig gets bigger and eats more.

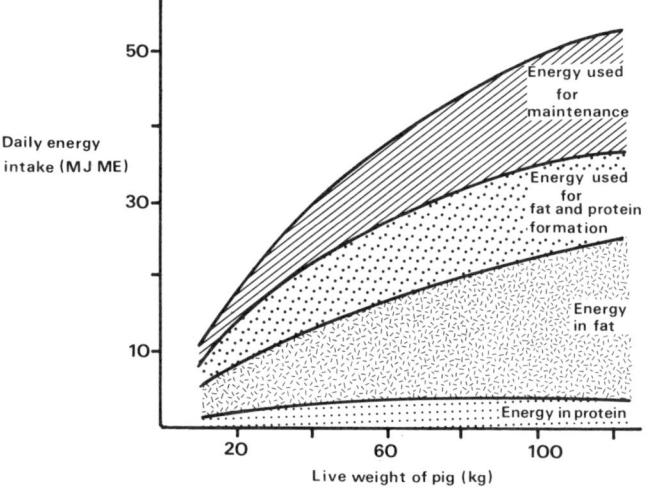

Figure 4.3. Daily gains of energy in the components of the body and daily losses of energy as heat in a growing pig.
Energy in protein and fat is stored in the body, energy used for fat and protein formation and for maintenance is lost from the body as heat.

Heat losses from the synthesis of new protein are more than thrice those from the synthesis of new fat (45 vs 14 MJ). This is because of restructuring to achieve the right balance of amino acids from out of the mixture supplied by the diet. Also, there is the energy cost of linking the amino acid units together to make up protein, this amounts to about 7·5 MJ ME/kg new protein formed. Lastly, and most important, for each increment of new protein made, about 4 to 12 times that amount is simply being recycled. Most of the energy expenditure in protein growth is not in the cost of the new growth itself, but in the much greater total cost of protein recycling. In this way, the expenditure of 7·5 MJ ME/kg for forming new protein can readily be raised at least sixfold to 45 MJ or more.

The protein mass is smaller in a lighter pig. Energy cost associated with recycling the protein mass is therefore less in a smaller pig than a larger one. Energy saving on account of less protein to cycle in the smaller pig is, however, partly offset by the cycle occurring faster in the younger animal. Nevertheless, it appears that the energy cost of protein synthesis (inclusive of the 24 MJ of energy contained within the protein) may increase as the animal grows; from about 45 MJ ME/kg protein at 20 kg liveweight to about 80 MJ ME at 100 kg. The average value is 69 MJ ME/kg.

In terms of new protein made per unit of protein mass to be recycled, the mammary gland is extremely efficient. Energy costs of protein synthesis by the mammary gland of sows has been estimated at 42 MJ ME/kg milk protein, which is nearly equivalent to the lowest value and well below the average value, for growing pigs.

Energy from protein

Only about 50 per cent of the digested protein goes into the formation of new protein growth. The energy in the remaining 50 per cent of digested protein is 24 MJ/kg, but this is not available until the nitrogen part is excreted. Deamination costs 2·2 MJ/kg protein and every g of nitrogen in urine takes with it 0·045 MJ. Further, protein is not as appropriate for use in the body as is glucose. This means that by the time the energy in protein has been released for use in the body some 12 MJ have been used up, leaving a yield of 11–12 MJ/kg protein deaminated.

Losses of protein are therefore turned to some good use in the energy economy. However, the deamination process is inefficient as a mechanism for creating energy and is usually not voluntarily resorted to as a means of energy supply. At 12 MJ/kg protein, the ME yield of a unit of protein is rather less than that of carbohydrate (about 16 MJ), so the price advantage would need to be in favour of protein—an unlikely eventuality.

Body water

The whole body of a 100 kg pig contains about 30 kg fat, 14 kg protein, 3 kg ash and 50 kg water. Water is the major component of the pig, with fat next. Water is the critical factor in the energetic efficiency of growth. Fatty tissue contains only about 10–15 per cent water; but lean contains about 70–80 per cent water. Clearly, as water costs practically nothing, the more water that can be put down in the body of the pig the more efficient growth will be. Whilst protein deposition is itself more costly in terms of energy than fat deposition, the live growth which results from that protein deposition is very much cheaper, because it is associated with water in the ratio of about 1 protein to 4 water in the form of lean meat.

Table 4.5 shows two rates of daily liveweight gain; 0·5 kg (slow) and 1·0 kg (fast). Each rate of gain is given a different proportion of lean to fat; 4 of lean : 1 of fat is very lean, 1 of lean: 1 of fat would be the type of ratio one could get in a bacon pig fed *ad libitum*. The different compositions of the gain bring about different energy costs for that gain; gain at the lean-to-fat ratio of 4:1 is much cheaper energetically than gain at the lean-to-fat ration of 1:1. The next step is to allow for the energy costs of maintenance, in the example given, 15 MJ of ME. In the last column is shown the total energy expended over the four example animals expressed per kilo of weight gain. In the case of both slow gain and fast gain the leaner gain is cheaper. Total energy costs also show how the faster growing pig is more efficient, even when the gain of that pig is very fat. It is the distribution of the overhead cost of maintenance which brings about this effect; for the slow-growing pig the same maintenance cost is spread over half the productive gain.

TABLE 4.5. Influence of leanness and of rate of gain upon the efficiency of energy use

Gain in weight (kg/day)	Lean: fat ratio	Composition of gain (g)			Energy for weight gain (MJ ME)	Energy for maintenance (100 kg pig) (MJ ME)	Total energy per kg weight gain (MJ ME)
		Protein	fat	water			
0·5	4:1	90	90	320	10·2	15	50·4
0·5	1:1	57	227	216	15·5	15	61·0
1·0	4:1	180	180	640	20·4	15	35·4
1·0	1:1	114	454	432	31·0	15	46·0

Control of body temperature

For the pig to function properly its body temperature must be maintained in the region of 39°C. Figure 4.3 shows how the pig is particularly good at casting off large quantities of heat into the atmosphere. Where the temperature difference between that of the pig and that of its environment is greater than can be bridged by the quantity of heat which the pig loses in the normal course of metabolism, the pig must react by generating more heat in its body. To produce this extra heat, food is diverted from more productive processes such as growth, and burnt up.

The amount of heat produced by pigs depends on their size and productivity (Table 4.6). Larger pigs have higher maintenance costs and produce more waste heat. Faster growing pigs also produce more heat than slower growing pigs. If a large rapidly growing pig is placed in the same environment as a small slow-growing pig, the large pig is better able to cope with a temperature deficit and is less likely to divert feed energy from productive processes to keep itself warm.

TABLE 4.6. Calculated heat production of pigs

	Heat produced (MJ/day)
20 kg pig growing 0·2 kg day	6·3
20 kg pig growing 1·0 kg day	15·0
100 kg pig growing 0·2 kg day	16·8
100 kg pig growing 1·0 kg day	24·4

Suggested temperatures at which food is diverted to keep the pig warm (the lower critical temperature or LCT) for pigs with different rates of heat output are given in Table 4.7.

TABLE 4.7. Lower critical temperatures (LCT) calculated for pigs with various rates of heat output

Heat output by pig (MJ/day)	LCT (°C)
5	25
10	21
15	17
20	14
25	10
30	7

For pigs growing at *average* rates, the heat output in MJ is close to the value for metabolic body weight in Appendix 1. Thus a pig of 20 kg with a metabolic body weight of 10 kg is likely to produce about 10 MJ of heat and have an LCT of 21°C. A pig of 80 kg with a metabolic body weight of 27 kg is likely to produce about 27 MJ of heat and have an LCT of 10°C. Faster growing pigs will produce more heat and have a lower LCT. Conversely, pigs growing slower than average will produce less heat output and have a higher LCT.

The difference between the house temperature and the LCT for any particular pig is the heat deficit which the pig must make up by burning up feed energy. On average about 0·016 MJ of ME is required daily for each kg of metabolic body weight for each degree

E

centrigrade difference between the LCT and the environmental temperature. For example, a 40 kg pig producing 15 MJ of heat from maintenance and productive processes and with a LCT of 17°C in an environment with an air temperature of 10°C will need to divert about 2 MJ ME per day from growth into heat production. This represents about 10 per cent of the animal's total energy consumption, which would otherwise have been used for growth.

Total energy supply and efficiency

Energy passing into the body goes first to satisfy the needs for gestation and milk production. Next are the maintenance needs. This order of priority may result in breeding animals failing to maintain themselves and losing liveweight in pregnancy and lactation. When the maintenance requirements for energy have been supplied, the remaining energy is available for the production of protein and fat. Although the ability of the pig to lay down protein is probably limited to a particular quantity each day, there is no such desire on the part of the growing pig to limit its rate of fat production. When the limit to the daily rate of protein synthesis is reached, and all the energy requirements for protein synthesis satisfied, the remaining energy is turned into body fat.

As growth of protein requires dietary energy, as well as dietary protein, it is possible for an energy shortage to hold up the growth of

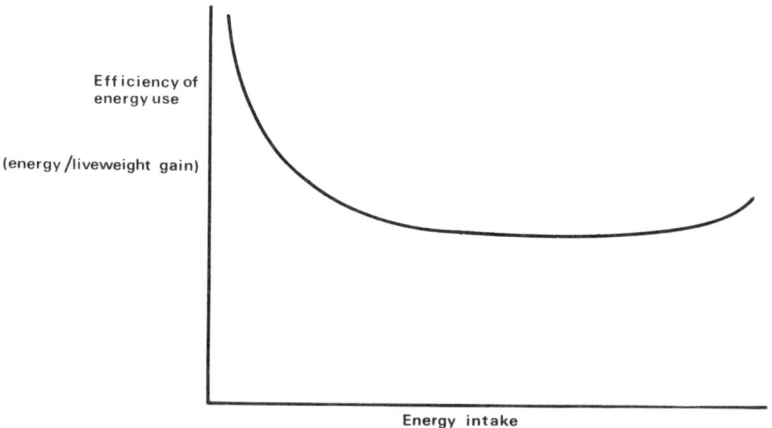

Figure 4.4. Effects of increasing daily energy intake upon the efficiency of energy use (energy intake/liveweight gain) for growth in the pig.

lean meat. This is particularly probable in young pigs when a limit to lean growth may often result from an energy deficit. In the young pig, appetite tends to restrict total energy supply, but the potential for lean growth is as great at 20 kg as at 120 kg.

When protein growth is maximised, then increasing the energy supply will increase growth rate by increasing fatness. An increase in growth rate will improve efficiency by reducing the effect of the maintenance loading, but simultaneously an increase in fatness will reduce efficiency of energy use on account of the low water content of fat as opposed to lean. The change in efficiency of energy use with increasing energy intake is represented in Figure 4.4. Efficiency improves as the cost of maintenance is spread over progressively more weight gain; subsequently, the benefits of spreading maintenance begin to be counteracted by the inefficiency of growth which is increasingly dominated by fat. Finally, the inefficiencies of fat production are sufficiently large for the overall efficiency of energy use to be noticeably worsened.

ENERGY REQUIREMENTS OF GROWING PIGS

Calculations to approximate energy requirements are given below; it is assumed that ME is 95 per cent of DE, lean is 77 per cent water and fatty tissue is 10 per cent water.

Maintenance—About 0·5 MJ DE/kg body weight$^{0.75}$
(metabolic body weight, Appendix I)

Lean growth—About 15 MJ DE/kg lean formed
(69 MJ ME/kg protein)

Fat growth —About 50 MJ DE/kg fatty tissue formed
(54 MJ ME/kg fat)

Cold —About 0·017 MJ DE/kg metabolic
body weight/°C of cold

EXAMPLE 1:

A 60 kg pig to grow at 600 g daily. Case (A), a dietary protein supply adequate for 80 g protein (350 g lean) growth daily. Case (B), a rate of growth of 100 g protein (450 g lean) daily.

(A) Maintenance : 60 kg; $W^{0.75}$ = 21·6 × 0·5 = 10·8 MJ DE
Lean : 0·350 × 15 = 5·3 MJ DE
Fat . : 600−350 = 250; 0·250 × 50 = 12·5 MJ DE

Requirement for energy   28·6 MJ DE

(B) Maintenance : 10·8 MJ DE
 Lean : 0·450 × 15 6·8 MJ DE
 Fat : 600–450 = 150; 0·150 × 50 7·5 MJ DE

Requirement for energy 25·1 MJ DE

EXAMPLE 2:
A 40 kg pig eats 2 kg of a diet of 13 MJ DE. Case (A), house Temperature 20°C. Case (B), house temperature 12°C. Protein supply allows 100 g protein (450 g lean) growth daily.

(A) Maintenance : 40 kg; $W^{0·75}$ = 15·9 × 0·5 = 8·0 MJ DE
 Lean : 0·450 × 15 = 6·8 MJ DE
 Fat : 26–(8·0 + 6·8) = 11·2/50 = 0·224 kg
 Rate of growth: 450 + 224 = 674 g daily.

(B) Approximate LCT = 18°C
 Maintenance : = 8·0 MJ DE
 Lean : = 6·8 MJ DE
 Cold : 18–12 = 6; 6 × 15·9 × 0·017 = 1·6 MJ DE
 Fat : 26–(8·0 + 6·8 + 1·6) = 9·6/50 = 0·192 kg
 Rate of growth: 450 + 192 = 642 g daily.

ENERGY USE BY PREGNANT SOWS

The energy economy of pregnancy is dominated by the biological adaptation of pregnancy anabolism. This phenomenon is demonstrated by feeding pregnant and non-pregnant sows the same amount of food. At the level of intake which will maintain a non-pregnant animal at constant body weight, the pregnant sow will produce a litter of piglets, all the associated membranes, her new mammary tissue, *and* a little extra weight gain for herself.

The composition of this maternal weight gain is not yet clear. It appears that in gilts it is mostly associated with water and protein, whereas in sows there are considerable amounts of fat laid down. These differences may relate to the gilt having higher body fat reserves than a sow in any case, and therefore having a rather lower demand for fat, but a greater need for protein growth, in her endeavour to attain her mature protein mass.

It appears that for the sow at any rate—rather than the gilt—the first 60 days of pregnancy are characterised by the deposition of quantities of fat, about 150 g daily, as well as 50 g or more of protein. In the second half of pregnancy the protein gains continue, but some of the fat is actually broken down, so there is a depletion of fatty tissue.

There is some evidence that the maintenance requirements for pregnant sows are reduced in early pregnancy, and it is in this way that energy is left over for fat deposition. Later, as the second half of pregnancy is entered, the 'heat of gestation' actually increases the maintenance needs. This increase in heat output is thought to result from the increased metabolic activity connected with the supply of nutrients to the foetuses, foetal growth and foetal protein recycling, and the catabolism of maternal fat depots.

Most of the tissue deposited in the uterus is protein and glycogen; lipid only reaches 1 per cent of the total. The energy costs of cycling foetal protein are unknown; but in view of the changing nature of the protein material in respect of the content of nucleic acids, and of the cell differentiation and reorganisation which are a unique feature of early embryonic and foetal growth, it is likely that protein cycling in the uterus is many times greater than in post-natal life. It is not surprising therefore that as the state of pregnancy progresses, heat losses from the sow increase.

ENERGY REQUIREMENTS OF PREGNANCY

As the foetal load is not particularly great, and only significant in the last 30 days of pregnancy, and as the sow has the additional remarkable facility of pregnancy anabolism, the energy requirements of pregnancy *per se* are, effectively, nil.

The necessary calculation is for the maintenance of the sow and for the extent of maternal liveweight gain required. Weight gain by the sow is a simple function of energy supply and is assumed to abide by the same rules described for growth in the younger animal.

In view of the degree of uncertainty which still surrounds the quantitative aspects of pregnancy, it would appear unwise to make any calculation of energy needs too sophisticated. It is possible to allow for a maintenance requirement of 0·40 MJ ME/kg $W^{0.75}$ (metabolic body weight) in early pregnancy, and 0·55 MJ ME/kg $W^{0.75}$ in late pregnancy, and to account separately for the energy costs of growing foetuses and mammary tissues. But it is probably more realistic, and certainly simpler, to use the maintenance costs already described for growing pigs—about 0·475 MJ ME or 0·5 MJ DE/kg $W^{0.75}$. Again, the composition of the sow gain is going to be very variable and to depend much upon the state of the sow in question. It is likely that sows carrying their second and subsequent litters will be leaner and more mature; they are therefore more likely to require fat deposition than protein growth. If the composition of sow gain is taken at an average of 15 per cent protein and 25 per cent fat, the energy cost is in the region of 25 MJ ME or 26 MJ DE/kg live maternal gain.

The maternal gain to be allowed in pregnancy will vary according to the state of the sow. Usually sows are fed the minimum commensurate with productivity, hence the objective in terms of sow size must be to smallness rather than largeness. On the other hand, the sow herself requires to make some growth. Firstly in her attempts to attain mature size, and secondly to provide herself with reserves to refurbish the coming lactation and ensure she is in a fit condition for re-mating at the end of lactation. Younger sows readily gain 60 kg in pregnancy. An average allowance would be for the sow to be 35 kg heavier at the end of pregnancy than she was at the beginning; of this, about 20 kg will be in the maternal tissues.

A sow gaining 20 kg in the course of a 115-day pregnancy would require $26 \times 20/115 = 4 \cdot 5$ MJ DE for this purpose daily. If she was to weigh 140 kg, her maintenance requirement would be 41 (see Appendix 1) $\times 0 \cdot 5 = 20 \cdot 5$ MJ DE. A total requirement of about 25 MJ DE daily.

ENERGY USE BY LACTATING SOWS

In common with the lactating cow, the sow is physiologically prepared to use body reserves of fat for the production of milk. Often the sow simply cannot eat enough to support a full lactation supplying the nutrient demands of a litter of eight or more piglets. The pattern of pregnancy weight gain has its natural antithesis of lactation weight loss. That this pattern of gain and loss is the natural order of things is supported by observations of voluntary feed intakes by lactating sows. Sows fed well in pregnancy, and being more fat at the beginning of lactation, will eat less food and lose weight faster than their companions fed on lower levels in pregnancy and reaching lactation in a less fat state.

The energetic efficiency of milk protein production is high—over 50 per cent. The total energy costs of milk protein synthesis are 40–45 MJ ME/kg milk protein. This value is about equivalent to that suggested for muscle growth in very young pigs, and much lower than the 70 MJ or more proposed for older pigs. Energy from dietary sources, reaching the blood stream as glucose and fatty acids, is converted into energy in milk in the form of lactose and milk fat, with an efficiency of about 65 per cent. The conversion of energy to body fat may be somewhat higher (say 75 per cent) and the conversion of body fat to milk energy higher still (say about 85 per cent). Overall, the double conversion of diet energy to body energy to milk energy is about 65 per cent; no different from the more direct conversion of diet energy to milk energy.

The energy content of sow's milk depends upon its composition, which averages about 6 per cent protein, 5 per cent lactose, and 8 per cent fat. The total energetic value is therefore 5·4 MJ/kg milk.

For sows with ample body reserves of fat, yield in the first 21 days of lactation is relatively uninfluenced by the dietary energy supply. When the sow uses body fat as an energy source of milk synthesis, it requires about 1·2 MJ of body fat energy to make 1 MJ milk energy (efficiency of 85 per cent); or 31 g body fat (39·3 MJ/kg fat), or 35 g of fatty tissue loss. As the efficiency of conversion of energy from dietery sources into milk energy is about 65 per cent, 1 MJ of milk energy would cost 1·5 MJ ME. Thirty-five grams of body weight loss by the lactating sow therefore yields 1 MJ of milk energy and spares 1·5 MJ of dietary ME. One kilogram of body weight loss will yield 28–29 MJ of milk energy and spare 44 MJ ME from dietary sources.

The energy economy of lactation revolves around the balance of lactation yield, body reserves, and food intake. Only if the demands of lactation are high, the food inadequate, *and* the body reserves low, will energy intake directly affect lactation. This combination of circumstances is most likely to arise in late lactation and in older sows. If the sow is fed on a nutritional regime which progressively depletes her reserves of body fat—as is commonly the case—then as she gets older her ability to buffer lactation against an inadequate dietary energy supply diminishes. The effects of energy intake on lactation yield are therefore particularly significant over the longer term; low energy intakes bringing about a reduction in lactation yield for the second and subsequent litters.

ENERGY REQUIREMENTS OF LACTATION

Milk production: 8·3 MJ ME/kg milk (5·4 MJ/kg milk converted with an efficiency of 65 per cent), or 8·8 MJ DE/kg milk

Maintenance: 0·475 MJ ME/kg $W^{0·75}$ (metabolic body weight, Appendix 1), or 0·5 MJ DE/kg $W^{0·75}$

Liveweight gain of fatty tissues: 50 MJ DE/kg gain

Liveweight loss of fatty tissues: saves 44 MJ ME or 47 MJ DE/kg loss

EXAMPLE 1:

Sow of 160 kg fed 5 kg of a diet with 13 MJ DE/kg, suckling 9 piglets and giving 7 kg milk daily.

Energy intake: 5 kg × 13 MJ = 65 MJ DE
Energy losses: Maintenance   — 45 × 0·5 = 22·5
              Milk production   — 7 × 8·8 = 61·6
                                              84·1

Energy deficit: 84·1 MJ−65 MJ = 19·1 MJ dietary DE equivalent daily

Liveweight loss expected: 19·1/47 = 406 g daily.

EXAMPLE 2:
Sow of 140 kg fed 6 kg of the same diet, suckling 8 piglets and giving 6·5 kg of milk daily.
Energy intake: 6 kg × 13 MJ = 78 MJ DE
Energy losses: Maintenance —41 × 0·5 = 20·5
             Milk production —6·5 × 8·8 = 57·2
                                              77·7

Energy surplus: 78 MJ − 77·7 MJ = 0·3 MJ
Weight stasis expected.

Chapter 5

MINERALS, VITAMINS AND WATER

MINERALS

ABOUT THREE-QUARTERS of the mineral mass of a pig's body is calcium and phosphorus. The remaining quarter is almost entirely potassium and sodium. The body also contains some magnesium and small but measurable quantities of iron, zinc and copper. Other mineral elements are contained at trace levels.

Calcium and phosphorus provide the framework which, with protein and fat, form the bones of the skeleton. The skeleton is needed to support the weight of the body and bears a fairly strict relationship to the mass of the muscle which is attached to it. Because of their involvement in growth, calcium and phosphorus are required by the young animal in relatively large amounts, and unless a feed source contains bones itself or has a high calcium and phosphorus content, these elements need to be specially added to the diet. Usually the calcium and phosphorus supplement is bonemeal (Ca and P), di-calcium phosphate (Ca and P) or calcium carbonate (Ca alone). Sodium and potassium are particularly important in the body fluids, which are again closely associated with the lean mass fraction of the body. Most of the other elements such as magnesium, iron, cobalt, iodine, copper manganese, selenium, fluorine, chlorine, molybdenum and zinc are only needed in small or minute quantities to maintain body function and to help drive along the metabolic processes.

Supplementation of diets

Apart from the unusual cases of calcium and phosphorus, for which there is a major dietary need, the mineral requirements of pigs are largely supplied by minerals occuring naturally in the feedstuffs which make up the pig's normal diet.

Our knowledge of the pig's use of mineral elements is limited. Where energy and protein resources are the most expensive part of the diet, there is some justification for blanket inclusion of levels of minerals found by practical experience to be adequate. This is not to say, of course, that chronic problems resulting from marginal deficiencies or marginal excesses may not occasionally arise as a result of this practice.

The mineral requirements of pigs are provided either by the normal levels in the feed ingredients or by the addition of a 'comprehensive' trace element mixture, or by special additions of feedingstuffs rich in those elements thought to be deficient. The usual practice is to supply by means of a trace-element supplement all the extra minerals which might be needed except calcium and phosphorus. The exclusion of these elements, which are the ones needed in large quantities, allows the trace supplement to be included at the low rate of 2–5 kg/tonne.

Mineral elements are required at very different levels. A rapidly growing pig, for example, needs the merest 10 mg of copper, but 20 g of calcium; a two thousand fold difference. A guide to levels of minerals currently included in pig diets is given in Table 5.1, from which it is evident that comparatively little is known about mineral needs of pigs. The aim of the mineral supplement should be to balance the total needs of the animals with the supply of elements already contained within the diet ingredients. In the absence of adequate knowledge of either pig needs or feed composition, this would appear no more than a fond hope.

There are two major problems in trying to ration minerals to pigs. Firstly, the amount the animal really needs has, to date, defied accurate definition. Secondly, it is difficult to determine the exact supply of available minerals to the pig from the natural feed ingredients.

Unlike a failure to supply adequate protein or energy, a deficiency of mineral is unlikely to be immediately apparent. When a diet is made from natural ingredients it is extremely difficult to produce symptoms of mineral deficiency in pigs. Further, minerals contribute to the general well-being of the animal, not to saleable products. When maximum meat production is the standard of assessment, the minimum need for a mineral by a growing pig is less than the need if general well being is the standard. The calcium and phosphorus requirement for bone strength is well above that for growth. If a pig is to go to slaughter at half its adult size and one-tenth its potential life span, what need has it for strong bones?

Some attempt has been made at recommending calcium and phosphorus allowances for pigs; these are given later in Chapter 11. For the other mineral elements, generally included in the trace-element mix, only some tentative conclusions can be drawn:

1. The supply of minerals must not reach toxic level. A particular watch should be kept of the possibility of heavy metal (for

example, copper), build-up in the bodies of breeding stock.
2. Adequate provision must be made to prevent overt deficiency symptoms and to ensure no loss of any aspect of production.
3. Between these two extremes, cost must be balanced with an insurance policy for the well-being of the animal. Mineral problems in pig herds are rare, but they *can* occur and occasionally reduce performance.
4. The normal feedstuff components of a conventional diet will supply adequate quantities of all minerals except calcium and phosphorus. Dietary supplementation with 'a trace element' mix is therefore not justifiable as a purposeful act to bridge a gap between the pigs needs and the diet supply—there is unlikely to be any such gap. Trace element mixes serve as insurances against the possible eventuality of a deficiency. Fortunately, the cost of the minerals is an insignificant proportion of total diet cost.

TABLE 5.1. Dietary inclusions of minerals per tonne of mixed air-dry diet

	Suggested in final mixed diet	Indicated as being provided in proprietary trace element supplements
Calcium (kg)	4-10	
Phosphorus (kg)	4-8	
Potassium (kg)	about 2·5	
Salt (Sodium Chloride) (kg)	0·5-3	2-3·5
Magnesium (g)	300-800	10-75
Iron (g)	about 60	50-400
Zinc (g)	40-100	40-140
Manganese (g)	5-40	20-60
Copper (g)	3-10	5-250[1]
Iodine (g)	some	1-4
Cobalt (g)	some	0·5-2

[1]Copper as a growth stimulant for growing pigs; usually at 175 g/t

Utilisation of the major minerals

Although the requirement for minerals is stated and supplied on the basis of a dietary concentration, pigs require minerals in particular daily quantities.

Minerals may be considered as being needed for purposes of both maintenance (refurbishing the losses resulting from the inefficiencies of the continual recycling of body tissues containing the various elements) and production. In the growing pig, the dietary need for the major minerals can be linked to the rate of growth. In Table 5.2 are some suggested values for minerals retained for each 100 g of protein growth (that is, about 450 g lean).

TABLE 5.2. Retentions for some mineral elements/100 g of protein deposited in growing pigs

	Retention of mineral, g/100 g protein deposited
Calcium	6-8
Phosphorus	2·5-4
Sodium	0·5-1
Potassium	1-2
Magnesium	0·1-0·3

As most commercial pigs *do* deposit about 100 g of protein per day, these values would be similar to a daily rate of mineral retention for an actively growing pig. To calculate the amount of mineral that should be supplied in the pig's diet, the rate of retention needs to be multiplied by the efficiency with which dietary mineral is retained. This efficiency is, of course, a function of the digestibility, or availability, of the mineral and the rate of excretion of mineral in the urine.

The different quantities of minerals recommended for pigs do not necessarily reflect the extent to which the pig uses that element. Even for a frequently used element, like iron, the daily supply might only need be quite small when the daily rate of retention of the element is low and where the economy of recycling in the animal is very efficient. In many cases, the ability of the intestines to re-absorb intestinal secretions of minerals is high, as is the ability of the kidney to filter and re-absorb mineral from the urine. When the intake of some minerals is increased, the efficiency of digestion is reduced, or the pig's losses raised, in compensation. By such means the animal can maintain itself in mineral balance over a range of dietary rates of supply. The extent of this range will differ with different minerals, and the form in which they are supplied.

Sodium and potassium

Both these elements are usually digested with an efficiency greater than 70 per cent. The urinary excretion is variable, and depends very much on the rate of dietary supply; absorption above the daily need results in a *pro rata* urinary loss. Sodium is usually supplied as the chloride (common salt) which also acts as an appetiser for diets. Where pigs are on a restricted water supply, salt toxicity might be possible if the diet contains above 1 per cent (10 kg/tonne). Ample potassium is usually available from normal vegetable diet ingredients. There is no need to supplement practical diets. Potatoes are particularly rich in potassium; a diet containing 50 per cent potato may have almost three times the potassium level of an all-cereal diet. There has been some argument as to whether potassium could cause wet droppings in poultry; in pigs, the only obvious effect of feeding potato in relation to potassium levels is a urinary potassium excretion elevated by the expected factor of 3 or 4.

Magnesium
Seventy per cent of the magnesium in the body is contained in bone. Magnesium can be very poorly used from a normal diet; probably little more than 25 per cent of diet magnesium is absorbed. Estimates of availability are, however, very variable, and high values have also been measured for this element. The body's need for magnesium is small, even in growth, and probably less than 10 per cent of that eaten is retained.

Phosphorus and calcium
Of the total body phosphorus 90 per cent is in bone, and of the total body calcium 99 per cent is in bone. The elements are co-precipitated in bone in the ratio of about 2 calcium:1 phosphorus forming hydroxy apatite. Phosphorus is rather poorly absorbed; usually around 50 per cent from a normal diet. The availability of dietary phosphorus depends considerably upon the source of the phosphorus. Inorganic phosphorus (particularly calcium phosphate in di-calcium phosphate and in bonemeal) is more digestible than organic sources. Plant phosphorus, three-quarters of which is phytate phosphorus, should be assumed to be less than 40 per cent available. Some rock phosphates are also unavailable; the alumino-ferric phosphates and soft phosphates, for example, are of low value. The body controls its phosphorus balance by the amount of phosphorus in the urine. This allows the pig some degree of adaptability to the vagaries of diet sources.

The calcium and phosphorus balance may affect the efficiencies of use of both elements. Calcium and phosphorus are needed in correct proportion to each other in order to lay down efficiently new calcium-phosphate in the skeleton. However, the body does have some powers of adjustment in relation to both calcium supply and phosphorus excretion rate. For serious disruption, it is probable that the ratio of calcium:phosphorus must really be quite wide—3:1 anyway. A ration no wider than 2:1 is suggested where vitamin D levels are marginal or where phosphorus levels are low.

The capability of the pig to excrete calcium in the urine is very limited, and only about 10 per cent of the absorbed calcium leaves the body in this way. This means that the control of body calcium is achieved at the point of absorption. If diet supply is too high, the availability will decrease. If diet supply is too low, it will increase. In a like manner, the greater needs of growing pigs will bring about a greater rate of absorption of calcium as compared with the rather lower needs for calcium of an adult pig. However, the extent to which any such increase can take place may well be limited by the source of dietary calcium and the ability of the intestine to absorb it. Normal values for calcium availability seem to range between 30 and 60 per cent.

VITAMINS

The formulation of diets containing adequate levels of vitamins has been revolutionised by the industrial preparation of vitamins which are stabilised to prevent deterioration during storage and which rarely react with other components of the diet. Synthetic vitamins have established an enviable record in purity of product, so that formulation to specified levels of supplemented vitamins is easily undertaken. On the other hand, the levels of vitamins in natural feedstuffs are variable and difficult to establish without complicated and expensive analyses. Consequently, great reliance has been placed in the use of a package of selected vitamins which supplies the *total* needs of these vitamins to the pigs. This practice can lead to excess levels since little reliance is placed on the natural vitamin content of feedstuffs; but only in the case of vitamin D is excess likely to lead to practical problems.

As is the case for the trace minerals, vitamins are added into pig diets in the form of a composite pre-mix, the vitamins supplied by the pre-mix providing for the daily needs of the pig when the recommended usage rate is adhered to. Vitamin and trace element supplements are available from a variety of manufacturers and are usually added to the diet at the rate of 2–5 kg/tonne.

The science of supplying potent vitamin sources to the pig has not been matched by the complementary experiments needed to identify what *level* of vitamin inclusion is required. In many cases the method of approach used has been to produce deficiency symptoms by means of unusual feedstuffs, and then to determine the response of the pig to supplementary synthetic vitamins. This approach does not reflect practical pig feeding conditions. In addition, the levels of vitamin inclusion required to eliminate specific dietary deficiencies, such as eye defects following low levels of vitamin A intake, may distract attention from the fact that complex processes such as reproduction may be affected marginally, but importantly, by the use of low levels over an extended period.

The producer must therefore accept that the nutritional adviser or the veterinary surgeon may be advising on vitamin requirements on the basis of all the available evidence, but may still be out by a factor of 10. Any comments concerning specific vitamin levels must be treated with respectful caution.

Lastly, there is no clear indication as to whether 'stress' affects vitamin needs, even if stress could be identified with accuracy.

FAT SOLUBLE VITAMINS

Vitamin A

Vitamin A is essential for the correct functioning of the eye and in the maintenance of the tissues forming the outer layers of mucous membrane of many systems such as the respiratory, reproductive and nervous systems. Where deficiency of vitamin A is produced experimentally, blindness, poor reproductive performance and lowered growth rate occur. One of the problems of vitamin nutrition is that such symptoms are not exclusive to vitamin A.

Vitamin A occurs in a number of forms, but fish oils are a particularly potent source; whilst plants contain the pro-vitamins A which are usually characterised as carotenoid pigments. The carotene can then be changed into vitamin A in the wall of the intestinal tract. It has been calculated that 1 mg of carotene (β) equals 560 international units (i.u.) of vitamin A. Different forms of carotene are connected with differing efficiencies and it is difficult to determine accurately the conversion of carotene in a feedstuff into vitamin A in the body of the pig. In addition, the presence of copper, vitamin E and nitrates all influence vitamin A availability and utilisation.

The requirements of pigs to exclude specific dietary deficiencies and to maintain acceptable growth and reproductive efficiency are supplied in Table 5.3. For all the vitamins listed in Table 5.3 the levels are expressed per tonne of mixed diet. The levels quoted in the table are heavily reliant upon the requirements recommended by the Agricultural Research Council.

Vitamin D

Vitamin D deficiency is usually characterised by muscular malfunction and these symptoms are followed by a distortion of bone growth which results from a disturbance of the normal calcification of the bone tissues, particularly the growing points of the long bones. These conditions often lead to rickets in young pigs and osteomalacia in older pigs.

Two forms of vitamin D are relevant to pig nutrition, vitamins D_2

and D_3. D_3 is found in animal tissues, whilst D_2 is formed when a substance found in some plant tissues (ergosterol) is irradiated naturally by ultra-violet light. Most cereal feedstuffs fed to pigs are, however, devoid in D_2.

The close relationship between vitamin D and calcium and phosphorus metabolism of the bones means that the level of vitamin D required is related to the levels of calcium and phosphorus supplied in the diets. Vitamin D supplied in excess can lead to poor growth rate and eventually to calcification of the heart, lungs and the kidneys.

The recommended levels in Table 5.3 are best estimates of the needs of growing pigs, and in the face of totally inadequate evidence it must be assumed that the needs of the sow in terms of concentration in the diet are similar to those of growing pigs.

Vitamin E

Vitamin E is a general name covering a number of different forms of tocopherols. It is one of the most important vitamins for pigs, in spite of the conflicting evidence that emerges from pig experiments. Vitamin E deficiency is most likely to occur where highly unsaturated oils are included in the diet, where vegetable oils are oxidised, or where the grain used has deteriorated by poor storage conditions such as overheating.

The symptoms of vitamin E deficiency closely relate to these which occur as a result of a deficiency of selenium (Se). It is incorrect to assume that selenium and vitamin E are interchangeable in the diet and that excess of one will compensate for a deficiency in the other. It is likely that an exact relationship will eventually be found which describes the optimum levels of both nutrients.

The symptoms following the supply of inadequate levels of vitamin E in pregnancy are embryonic mortality and the production of weak, inco-ordinated pigs at birth. In lactation, low levels in the milk may produce in the piglets muscular inco-ordination, susceptability to suffer from shock when injected with iron and so-called 'White Pig Disease'. In the case of growing pigs, deficiencies may lead to muscular dystrophy.

The vitamin occurs naturally in green forages and high quality cereals which have been satisfactorily stored. Several forms of the vitamin occur, of which the alpha form (α-tocopherol) is the most biologically active. Many of the forms of vitamin E have low potency and availability and therefore care has to be used in the use of the general term 'total tocopherols' or 'vitamin E'. One international unit of vitamin E relates to the activity of one specific form of α-tocopherol that is particularly potent for pigs.

TABLE 5.3. Vitamin requirements of pigs

Vitamin	Liveweight and type of pig	Required per tonne of mixed dry diet	Comments	Normally provided as a supplement[1]
Vitamin A	up to 20 kg	1·4 million i.u. or 2·5 g β carotene		yes
	20–60 kg	1·6 million i.u. or 2·9 g β carotene		yes
	60–100 kg	1·9 million i.u. or 3·4 g β carotene		yes
	sows	6·0 million i.u. or 10·7 g β carotene		yes
Vitamin D	all stock	0·2 million i.u.	based on information for growing pig	yes
Vitamin E	all stock	10 thousand i.u.	especially needed where diet contains oil or grain of poor quality	yes if comments apply
Vitamin K	baby pigs	60 mg	no requirement established for older pigs	sometimes
Thiamine	up to 100 kg	1·5 g	no requirement established for sows	no
Riboflavine	up to 100 kg	2·5 g		sometimes
	sows	3·0 g		sometimes
Nicotinic acid	up to 20 kg	20 g	no requirement established for sows	sometimes
Pantothenic acid	up to 100 kg	10 g		yes
	sows	10 g		yes
Pyridoxine	up to 100 kg	2·5 g		no
	sows	1·0 g		no
Vitamin B_{12}	up to 20 kg	18 mg		yes
	20–100 kg	10 mg		sometimes
	sows	15 mg		yes
Choline	up to 100 kg	850 g	no requirement established for sows	no
Biotin				
Folic acid	Dietary estimates not established			no
Inositol				
Vitamin C				

[1] Where the vitamin is not normally provided in a vitamin and trace element supplement it is assumed that the other diet ingredients supply ample of the vitamin from natural sources.

The latest evidence (Table 5.3) is that up to 11 i.u. vitamin E should be added to each kg of diet, and that under exceptional circumstances the levels given as a therapeutic dose may be considerably higher. It is likely that vitamin E deficiencies will occur in specific dietary situations where grains are stored badly and where use is made of oil as a feedstuff. These levels are much higher than those traditionally recommended in UK and reflect the view that vitamin E supplementation, although allowing a variable response, has led to substantial practical advantages in a range of conditions.

Vitamin K

Vitamin K is closely associated with the mechanism for clotting blood, and deficiency of vitamin K leads to anaemia, navel bleeding of young pigs and general weakness.

Vitamin K occurs naturally in green plants, in animal products and in micro-organisms, and it would be expected that deficiency symptoms would not usually occur. However, the deficiency has been produced in pigs fed on mouldy grain and where the normal development of the microbial population of the alimentary tract has been prevented. The probability of these circumstances cannot be calculated, and low concentrations of vitamin K should be included into diets to minimise the possibility of a deficiency, which is of particular importance with regard to baby pigs.

WATER-SOLUBLE VITAMINS

The water-soluble vitamins, embracing the B complex and vitamin C, are important for animal metabolism. For many of these vitamins, natural feedstuffs contain sufficient concentrations to preclude the appearance under normal circumstances, of deficiency symptoms. In addition, there is the likelihood that intestinal synthesis of vitamins by the microbes of the alimentary tract can satisfy the requirements of the pig. In particular the needs of the pigs for biotin, folic acid, inositol and vitamin C can, under most circumstances, be produced either by synthesis in the intestine of biotin and folic acid or synthesis in the tissues of inositol and vitamin C. Even in those circumstances where absorption of the vitamins via the the intestine is not efficient, there is the possibility that if the pig has access to its own faeces it can satisfy its vitamin needs.

As the water-soluble vitamins are of particular importance in the metabolic processes, deficiencies result in a reduction in overall metabolic activity, which reduces growth rate and feed conversion efficiency, and also feed intake. The lack of characteristic symptoms for these reductions in general productive efficiency means that a specific deficiency may not be recognised for some time. This difficulty can best be overcome by adopting a policy of ensuring that the levels of those vitamins not normally synthesised by the pig meet standards that ensure adequate growth rates.

Thiamine

The data on this vitamin is inadequate, although a deficiency under most conventional conditions is unlikely. The estimate that all pigs require about 1·5 g/tonne of dry feed (Table 5.3) seems under these circumstances to be a guess that cannot be disputed by objective evidence.

Riboflavine

A deficiency of riboflavine results in a general reduction in growth rate. Although it is possible under most circumstances that about 2 g riboflavine per tonne of dry feed is sufficient for young pigs; for pigs exposed to stress and for sows, a level of 3 g riboflavine it is suggested.

Nicotinic acid

This vitamin is used in enzyme systems, and a deficiency results in reduced growth, dermatitis and diarrhoea. Most of the nicotinic acid in cereal grains and maize is not in a form available to the pig. Fortunately, however, the pig can convert the amino acid tryptophan to nicotinic acid; 50 mg tryptophan being converted to 1 mg nicotinic acid.

In diets adequate in tryptophan a nicotinic acid deficiency is unlikely, but a requirement of 20 g/tonne of dry diet is suggested for young pigs as these are more likely to be at risk.

Pantothenic acid

Pantothenic acid is important to general metabolism. A deficiency may therefore have a systematic effect on productivity; quite apart from the characteristic pattern of inco-ordination of the hind legs which is due to degeneration of nervous tissue.

Pantothenic acid is a variable component of feeds; for example, it is present in abundance in groundnut meal. It is usually added to diets as a supplement in the form of calcium pantothenate which contains 92 per cent of available pantothenic acid. Pantothenic acid deficiency has been reported in UK using conventional feedstuffs, so it is essential to include supplementary pantothenic acid into pig diets.

Pyridoxine

Pyridoxine is similar to thiamine in its general action and presence in feedstuffs. Evidence from case histories suggest that pyridoxine levels could be increased.

Cobalamine (B_{12})

This vitamin contains traces of cobalt and therefore absolute deficiency of cobalt also results in B_{12} deficiency. B_{12} deficiency, apart from non-specific reductions in growth rate, can also lead to increased post-natal mortality.

Most feedstuffs of *animal* origin contain B_{12}, although as a variable component. Normally the intestinal synthesis of B_{12} is sufficient for the pig's needs.

Choline

The requirement for choline is closely related to the level of methionine in the diet since choline can be formed from the amino acid methionine. Clinical symptoms found in young pigs suffering from choline deficiency are unthriftiness, splay legs, and increased post-natal mortality. For sows, the indefinite symptoms of poor conception and poor lactation are often quoted on the basis of totally inadequate evidence. The requirements in Table 5.3 are therefore only approximate estimates.

Biotin

The symptoms of biotin deficiency include inco-ordination in the legs (particularly the hind legs) and cracks in the feet. These symptoms can be produced by the addition of drugs which prevent microbial activity in the intestine, or by the supply of synthetic diets using abnormal feedstuffs specifically deficient in biotin. Biotin deficiency can also occur following the feeding of grain which has been stored at high moisture content. There is a growing awareness that biotin levels should be more carefully considered than in the past.

Folic acid and Inositol

It is assumed for the present that circumstances where there is a specific dietary requirement for these vitamins are unlikely to occur.

Vitamin C

Under most circumstances the pig synthesises its need for vitamin C within its tissues and only in the case of young pigs kept under conditions considered to cause stress have deficiencies occurred. In these circumstances the addition of ascorbic acid has been advocated, but its presence as a normal component of pig diets outside of these exceptional circumstances cannot be justified.

WATER

The animal's need for water is paramount. Water is used for a variety of functions: as a transporting fluid in the body; to clear waste products from the body via the urine; to maintain the ionic balance of minerals in solution in the body; for use in chemical reactions involving water; as a medium within which the chemical reactions of the body can take place; to ease the passage of food materials down the alimentary tract; to lubricate joints, etc; to fill out the cells of soft tissues and so maintain the shape of the body; to help heat regulation by sweating and loss of water vapour from the surface of the lungs; and to incorporate into animal products such as lean meat, milk and foetuses.

The above is a formidable list; however, very little attention is usually given to water requirements. This is because in most circumstances water is inexpensive and the pig is particularly adept at balancing its own requirements.

The water content of the pig changes in relation to the composition of the body, lean containing very much more water than fat. A newborn pig contains about 80 per cent water, and by 100 kg this has reduced to 50 per cent of water. For a pig of any particular combination of tissues, however, the water content of the body is very stable. Thus, over a wide range of water intakes there is little change in the composition of the body.

Water balance is achieved by the kidney, which excretes water in direct proportion to water intake and water use within the body. The water excreted daily in urine can vary greatly and a wide range of rates of water passage are readily accepted by the kidney, although the animal will normally attempt to adjust its water intake to produce the appropriate strength of urine.

There is a minimum requirement for water without which the welfare of the pig would be adversely affected. This relates to the rate of loss of water vapour from the lungs, the amount of milk secreted, the need for fluids to clear toxins from the blood, the level of protein being deaminated, and the water content of the faeces. The temperature of the environment will influence water loss from the lungs, and the number of piglets sucking will affect the water losses in milk. Feeding high levels of protein, particularly if it is of low biological value, will increase the need for water to clear urea from the system in dilute solution in the urine. The ill effects of diarrhoea are primarily those of dehydration as a result of water losses in faeces, and it is essential that water intake is sufficient to replenish these losses. The need for water to clear toxins is exemplified in cases of ingestion of excess of salt, which may be treated with an ample supply of water to allow the pig to excrete sodium in dilute solution in the urine.

There is little reason to consider a maximum value for the level of water intake. The ingestion of water is unlikely to be forced, and the pig is unlikely purposefully to drink to the extent of self-creating its distress. There is a possibility that high intakes of water might bring about increased secretion of useful nutrients in the urine, for example of some mineral elements or of nitrogen, but there is no firm evidence for this.

A common feature of water ingestion by pigs is that it varies greatly from day to day and between individual pigs. The reason for these wide variations is not clear.

Frequency of provision of water

The frequency of drinking depends upon the dryness of the food (which relates the need for water in the mouth and alimentary tract), and to the frequency of water loss from the body. Lactating sows are suckled hourly and probably need to drink more frequently than pregnant sows. Pigs in hot temperatures must replenish water losses frequently to avoid dehydration, as must pigs which have diarrhoea. Younger animals tend to urinate more frequently.

Other uses for water

Water is useful for purposes other than as a body fluid, thus when water is added to dry feed it increases the rate of eating, and reduces wastage and dust. Young pigs like to eat dry feed together with water and will alternate between the source of feed and the water trough. If eaten fresh, the addition of water to the diet also increases its palatability.

TABLE 5.4. An approximate guide to daily water allowances for pigs

Pig type	Minimum water (kg/day)	Water-to-feed ratio (water:feed)	Minimum frequency of water provision (times/day)
Sucking piglets	ad libitum	—	freely available
Weaned piglets	ad libitum	—	freely available
Growing pigs (20-100 kg)	1-6[1]	2:1[2]	once or twice[3]
Pregnant sows	4	2·5:1	once or twice[3]
Lactating sows	12-21[4]	3:1	twice, but preferably freely available

[1] Depending upon liveweight of pig

[2] When water is used in pipeline feeding systems various ratios may be found, but often about 3:1

[3] Fattening pigs which are rationed and pregnant sows are often fed only once daily. These pigs may need access to water twice daily

[4] Depending upon the number of piglets sucking

Water allowances
The range of possible water intakes between the minimum and maximum levels is wide, and no firm suggestions regarding the amounts of water a pig should be given can be made. Table 5.4 merely serves as an approximate guide.

Chapter 6

APPETITE

THE AMOUNT of food a pig eats depends mainly upon its size and needs. Next to these, appetite is influenced by the digestibility of the diet, the energy density of the diet, its physical form and method of presentation, its palatability, and the environment of the pig.

Figure 6.1 is proposed as a guide to the probable limits to feed intake for pigs as they grow from 20–120 kg. In the case of the growing pig the animal's idea of the energy it needs is rather greater than that held by the feeder. It is every pig's ambition to be obese, and he will pursue this ambition with considerable determination. The point has to come, however, when even the pig realises that enough is enough; the presence of large stores of body fat finally register, and feed intake is accordingly reduced. The energy needs of the pig will also relate to the temperature of its environment and the demands for food energy to supply heat to keep the body warm. In colder environments, therefore, the appetite of pigs will increase to accommodate the greater need.

Given free access to food, pigs will tend to 'eat to energy'; that is, they will eat sufficient to satisfy energy needs, rather than eat a particular quantity of diet. Possible limits to the energy intake of growing pigs in terms of MJ of digestible energy daily are shown in Figure 6.2. The phenomenon of eating to energy results in the pig eating more food as the energy density (MJ DE/kg diet) of the diet decreases. Conversely, if the diet is made richer in energy the pig will eat proportionately less of it. The capacity of the pig to adjust in this manner is limited when a feed becomes of such low energy concentration that the pig is physically filled up before the desired MJ of energy are taken in. These responses are depicted in Figure 6.3. (A) shows energy intake increasing with energy concentration of the diet while the animal eats to its maximum physical capacity, then as energy concentration increases further, the capacity limit ceases to be the controlling mechanism and the animal begins to reduce the quantity of food eaten in order to maintain a steady daily supply of energy. The feed intake pattern which relates to this energy intake pattern is given in (B). Example (B) may not invariably apply, for

APPETITE

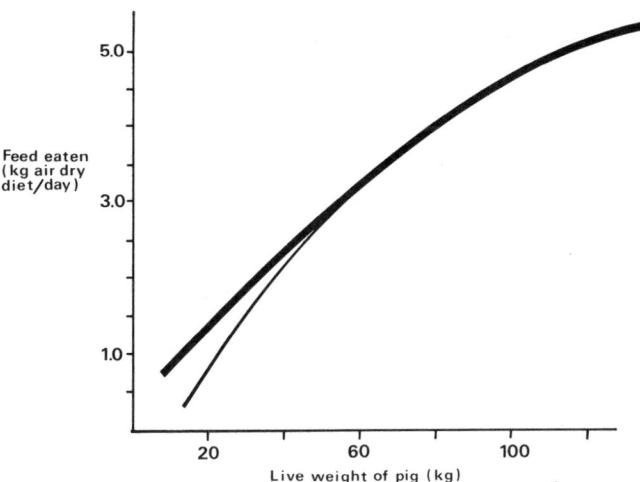

Figure 6.1. Suggested limits to quantity of feed which can be eaten daily by growing pigs. The thick line represents ideal conditions, the thinner line the probable limits to intake in commercial circumstances.

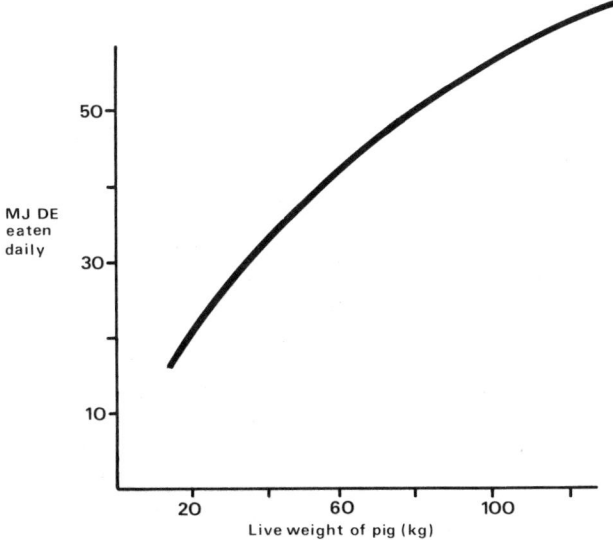

Figure 6.2. Possible limits to the energy intake (DE) of growing pigs.

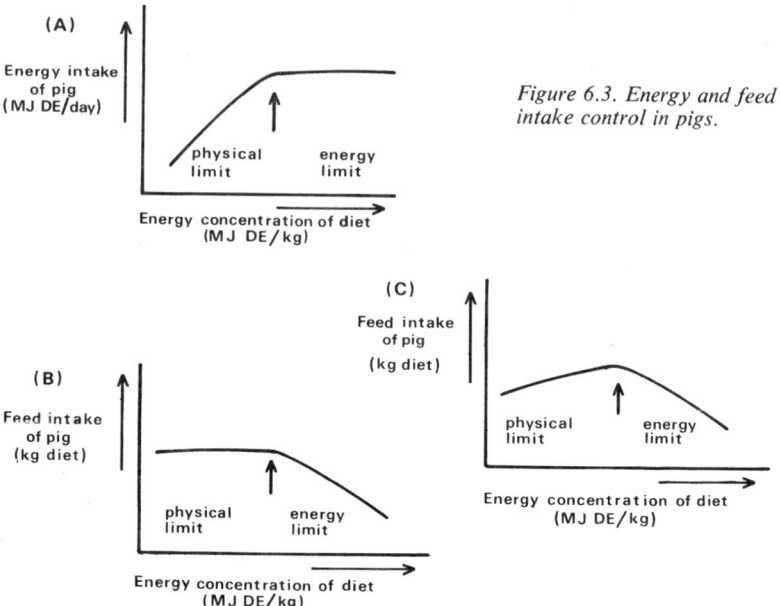

Figure 6.3. Energy and feed intake control in pigs.

when the quality of a feed improves, the physical limit to the amount of it which the alimentary tract can hold also increases; this relates to the increased rate of passage of better quality feeds through the intestines. A pig might only eat 3 kg of old grass, but 4 kg of weatings, although both might supply less than the energy need. In these cases the responses shown in (C) would apply.

Diet dilution

The possibility of rationing pigs while feeding them *ad libitum* to appetite holds considerable attractions. The theory is to dilute the diet so that the pig's physical capacity is achieved and the pig eats less energy. One problem is that the pig merely increases its intake to eat to energy and compensates for the dilution of the diet. This goes on until the gut-fill stage is reached, after which the pig's intake is progressively reduced by each increase in dilution rate. Dilution can be achieved by use of feedstuffs which are of low digestibility and high bulk such as weatings, oats, grass meal and the like or by the addition to the diet of completely indigestible materials such as sawdust, sand, vermiculite or vegetable fibres. Rationing pigs in this way has never gained much popularity. This is because the diluent itself costs money, and at least 20 per cent of the diet has to be diluted before significant effects are noticed, Further, as the diluent all ends up in the faeces, the slurry problem in increased.

Water may also serve as a dietary diluent. The pig can adjust for water and equalise dry-matter intake up to water concentrations of about 5 water:1 feed, but at 6:1 or above the volume of water in the pig is sufficiently great to reduce feed intake. Pipe-line and river-feeding systems allow possibilities for water dilution of diets.

Stress

The usual problem with pigs is an excessive appetite in relation to the carcase-quality penalties for over-fatness. However, under commercial conditions the 15–40 kg pig invariably fails to consume the amount of food he is capable of absorbing. For example, under carefully controlled conditions, 15 kg pigs can consume at least 1 kg of diet to grow at 500 g/day; a performance not mirrored in most commercial units.

Piglets under stress eat less feed; they become pernickety. Intake is reduced if pellets are too hard, if feed is stale or damp, if unpalatable diet constituents are included, if the diet is changed, or even if an ingredient of the diet is changed. Stress may be the result of removal from the sow, change of environmental conditions, change of pen, mixing with other pigs, introduction of strange pigs, or disease. Some or all of these conditions of stress, method feeding and diet apply to commercial pigs between 10 and 40 kg (20 and 90 lb), and sometimes again at 50 or 60 kg (120 lb). The thick line in Figure 6.1 is therefore unlikely to pertain in most real-life situations, and a more realistic limit to the amount of feed a pig can eat between 15 and 60 kg is given in Figure 6.1 by the thinner of the two lines.

Occasionally, a reduction in feed intake in the post-weaning phase may be an advantage. In some systems, feed is actually restricted following weaning. In particular, early-weaned pigs can over-eat and suffer diarrhoea. Older weaned pigs over-eating in the early stages of fattening may be more prone to gastro-enteritis and bowel oedema. In view of the potential lean growth that can be lost by reduced intake in the young pig, the decision to actively curtail intake in this stage of growth must depend upon the incidence of these disease problems in particular pig units.

Sows

Appetite in sows is further influenced by their body resources of fat and by the states of pregnancy and lactation.

Pregnant sows will eat more than non-pregnant sows of the same weight. In practice, intakes imposed with conventional diets are far below appetite limits; pregnant sows can eat 5–6 kg of diet but are usually fed about 2 kg. The appetite limit is of greater importance if diets of low energy density, such as those containing grass products, are contemplated for pregnant sows.

Lactating sows eat less if they have been liberally fed in pregnancy. The reduction in feed intake probably reflects the presence of ample body stores of fat which, when broken down, serve as a non-dietary source of nutrients for milk production. As sows age, fat reserves are depleted. First litter gilts will consume approximately 1 kg of feed less than sows suckling their second and subsequent litters.

Feed intake is also linked to milk production, higher rates of production bringing about an increased need for nutrients and an increased appetite to allow their ingestion. As milk yield by sows relates to the number of piglets sucking, the expected appetite of sows can be estimated from the litter size. Lactating sows in average condition with 5 piglets or less will eat at least 4·5 kg of diet daily, regardless of litter size. To this can be added about 0·25 kg for each piglet in the litter above 5, thus a sow with a litter of 8 or 9 piglets will eat about 5·5 kg and a sow with 12 or 13 piglets about 6·5 kg. A lactating sow is unlikely to eat more than 7 kg daily.

In the first few days of lactation the sow will eat less than the calculated amount. As milk yield is not yet established, the demands are low and body reserves are at their highest. Further, the sow will take a day or two to recover from the stresses of farrowing. Appetite usually builds up to full-feeding in the first five days or so of the lactation.

Frequency of feeding

The amount of food that can be eaten in a single meal is limited. Where intake requires to be maximised, increased frequency of feeding will increase intake. However, in the case of most growing pigs of more than 50 kg liveweight, and also pregnant sows, the ration allowance is usually much less than appetite and will be readily eaten in a single daily meal if conventional cereal-based diets are used.

It is not likely that a lactating sow will consume her feed requirement at one meal. Similarly, young growing pigs are likely to be induced to eat more if fed more than once daily, or if food is available *ad lib*. *Ad lib* feeding does not always maximise feed intake. If food is allowed to go stale, if the trough space is inadequate, if there is competition for the food or if the pigs lose interest in the food, then the provision of a number of discrete meals can bring about a greater intake than the continual availability of feed.

Chapter 7

RATIONING

THE RATION is the amount of feed offered to the pig daily, so rationing controls the intake of energy and protein by pigs. It is both the most simple and the most powerful method for controlling pig production. The amount of feed rationed influences all aspects of production and all the saleable products from the unit.

Because of this, rationing schemes used by individual producers should be individualistic. It is most unlikely that rations found satisfactory for one unit, in one set of circumstances, at one moment in time, will be satisfactory for that unit at any other time or for any other unit.

As the most potent tool for manipulating growth, production and profit, the rationing schemes used on the unit should be under constant review.

GROWING PIGS

As pigs grow they require more feed daily because their increasingly large bodies require additional amounts of energy for maintenance. As appetite increases with size as well, it is also possible to augment the rate of fat deposition. The potential for increasing the rate of lean growth is, as has been described, much more limited.

The growth of young pigs is usually restricted by a limited appetite. Further, food consumed by young pigs is very economically used, first because the maintenance cost is low, and second because most of the growth is as lean meat. For young pigs, therefore, not only are palatable, nutrient-dense diets prepared, but the pigs are encouraged to eat as much as possible.

At some point in the course of its growth the pig is usually rationed. Controlling feed intake will bring about a reduction in rate of gain and a decrease in fat synthesis, the degree of feed restriction regulating the extent of the change in growth rate and fatness. As growth rate is a positive attribute, growth will only be forgone if a greater benefit accrues through reducing fatness and improving grade. The ration scale used will depend upon the relative importances attributed to growth-rate and grade.

The weight at which feed restriction is imposed will depend upon the type of pigs being fed. Pigs which are prone to fatness and which have large appetites must be restricted at a lower weight than pigs which tend to grow lean rather than fat and have smaller appetites.

Feeding scales

There are, of course, an infinite number of possible feeding scales, but some examples are shown in Figure 7.1 and Table 7.1. Scale A represents a generous scale, of *ad lib* feeding to 60 kg, followed by liberal feeding to slaughter. Scale B, *ad lib* to 50 kg followed by a moderately liberal (B1) or a restrictive (B2) regime. Some fattening units operate a more simple scheme (C), whereby pigs feed to appetite until they are eating a set amount daily (2·5 kg, 3·0 kg or as thought appropriate), upon which they are restricted to that amount until slaughter. Pigs offered scale D are restricted from 20 kg liveweight. In many circumstances scales based on D rather than A may be the more appropriate; for example, D and type C might be combined, and so on.

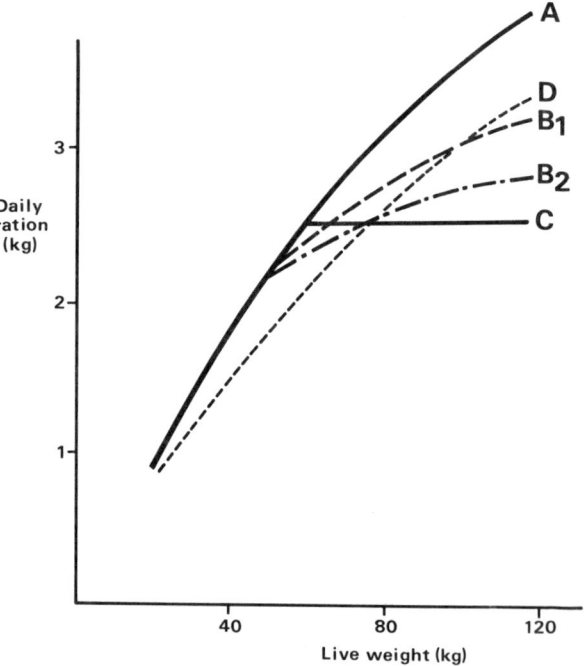

Figure 7.1. Examples of weight-based ration scales for growing pigs. The amount of nutrients fed on each scale will depend upon the density of the diet used.

TABLE 7.1 Ration scales for growing pigs

Weight of pig		Amount fed (kg)					Example regime if Scale B2 adjusted every 14 days[1]
(kg)	(lb)	Scale A	Scale B1	Scale B2	Scale C	Scale D	
20	44	1·0	1·0	1·0	1·0	0·8	1·0
25	55	1·2	1·2	1·2	1·2	1·0	
30	66	1·4	1·4	1·4	1·4	1·2	1·3
35	77	1·6	1·6	1·6	1·6	1·4	1·6
40	88	1·8	1·8	1·8	1·8	1·5	
45	99	2·0	2·0	2·0	2·0	1·7	2·0
50	110	2·2	2·2	2·2	2·2	1·8	2·2
55	121	2·4	2·3	2·3	2·4	2·0	
60	132	2·5	2·4	2·4	2·5	2·1	2·4
65	143	2·7	2·5	2·4	2·5	2·3	
70	154	2·8	2·6	2·5	2·5	2·4	2·5
75	165	3·0	2·7	2·5	2·5	2·5	2·5
80	176	3·1	2·8	2·6	2·5	2·6	
85	187	3·3	2·9	2·6	2·5	2·7	2·6
90	198	3·4	3·0	2·7	2·5	2·8	2·7
95	209	3·5	3·0	2·7	2·5	2·9	
100	220	3·6	3·1	2·8	2·5	3·0	
105	231	3·7	3·1	2·8	2·5	3·1	
110	242	3·8	3·2	2·8	2·5	3·2	

[1] Pigs growing about 575 g daily, for explanation see text.

Naturally, to achieve the same intake of nutrients, ration scales for higher density diets must be lower, and scales for lower density diets must be higher. To feed a higher density diet on the same scale is tantamount to increasing the scale.

Ad libitum

Young pigs can benefit from *ad lib* feeding. 'Young' in this sense refers to their degree of maturity. Late-maturing animals will be younger than early-maturing animals at the same weight. In consequence, some late-maturing pigs, particularly if they also have small appetites, may continue to give economical lean growth responses to *ad lib* feeding right up to 100 kg.

When a pig is rationed it must be fed daily with measured quantities of food. *Ad lib* feeding has advantages in terms of labour use and simplicity of management. Pigs fed all they can eat also maximise their rate of growth. The growth obtained may, however, be over-fat for the grade requirements. Appetite feeding is optimum for total growth but not necessarily optimum for lean:fat ratio in the growth.

Few strains of pigs *do* have sufficiently small appetites in relation to their potential lean growth to avoid over-fatness at 100 kg. At lower live weights although appetite is reduced, the potential for lean growth is not; so *ad lib* feeding is likely to be progressively more opportune as the market concerned is for lower slaughter weights. Pork pigs slaughtered at 60 kg (130 lb) are more often fed to appetite than those slaughtered at 70 kg (154 lb). Bacon pigs killed at 90–100 kg are invariably rationed.

Rationing steps: rationing by weight and by time

Many ration scales are related to the weight of the pig; the examples given in Table 7.1 relate to continuous scales with 5 kg intervals. Pigs can be weighed regularly to be allocated their appropriate ration, or weighed irregularly with intervening weight guestimates. The ration can be changed at any weight; 2, 5, 10 or 20 kg intervals, for example. Or at some set time interval; daily, weekly, fortnightly or monthly. If the ration was to be adjusted every 14 days, a stepwise ration regime would result. If the pigs grew at about 575 g daily or 8 kg in 14 days, the actual rationing regime offered to pigs on scale B2 would be similar to that given in the last column of Table 7.1. In each case the ration is chosen from the scale on the basis of the pig's current weight or the time interval which has lapsed. The weight or time interval chosen rather depends on the flexibility of the rationing system, the need for simplified management and one's faith in compensatory protein growth.

Pigs are often weighed merely to satisfy the need for current liveweight information for a weight-based feeding scale. But pig growth is reasonably predictable and largely dependent upon level of feeding; rationing is the propulsive force *for* growth, not the result *of* it. Accordingly, feeding scales can be time-based rather than weight-based. In the time-based scale the ration allowance is increased at the selected interval of time regardless of the weight of the pigs. The most simple one is 2·0 kg for the first 30 days of fattening (starting at 30 kg), 2·5 kg for the next 30 days and 3·0 kg thereafter. A more conventional scheme might be to start with a ration of 1·75 kg for a 30 kg pig and raise by 0·25 kg each fortnight till 3·25 kg (or any other pre-determined maximum) is reached.

In common with weight-based scales, time-based scales can be devised for pigs to grow slow or fast, fat or thin, depending upon the individual requirements of the feeder. For the more restrictive scales, pigs will, of course, be older at a given weight. The pig will grow according to the nutrients it receives, not the method used to ration it.

Choice of scale

The ration scale will depend on individual circumstances. There is nothing to be gained from any recommended scale; by trial (and error) is the best way to ascertain the most appropriate. The ration will change as circumstances change; high level feeding may be most profitable one year and low level feeding most profitable the next. It is hoped that the following chapters on choosing feeding programs will give some guide, but ultimately the ration scale is a matter of individual preference.

Observing the responses of pigs to ration scale in terms of days to bacon and carcass grade is a most enlightening, and financially rewarding, on-farm exercise. Rather more rewarding, one might suggest, than protracted musings over breeding records for purposes of gilt selection.

Rationing different sexes

The most important differences between the sexes are shown in their rates of deposition of lean meat. Thus the maxumum rates for daily protein deposition have been suggested as 90 g, 120 g and 135 g for castrates, gilts and boars, in that order (Table 2.3).

The nutritional demands of the growing boar are not well known. Ignorance has been highlighted in boar-testing stations—which diet should be used at what scale of rationing? The possibility of producing meat from boars is an attractive propostion and may generate interest in the special problems of feeding boars.

Continued on page 100

RATIONS

5. Young growers are often fed ad lib.

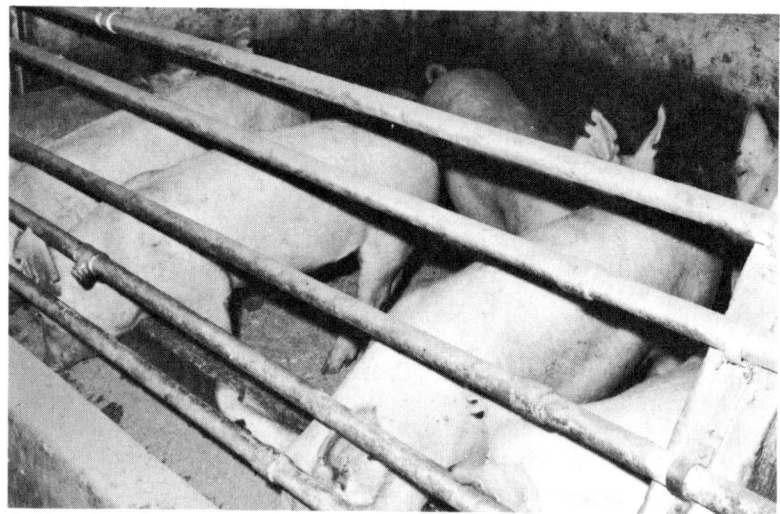

6. Fattening pigs are usually rationed to a scale, according to weight or age.

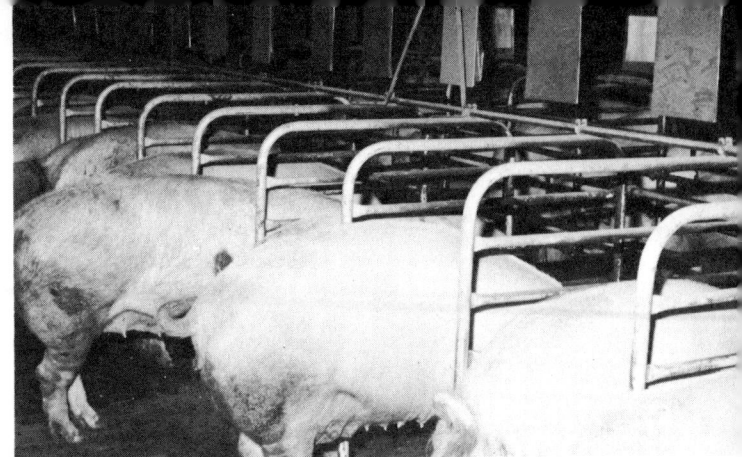

7. Individual feeding allows ration control for pregnant sows.

8. Group feeding, with the sow to the rear in trouble.

9. Group housing, but individual feeding; the feeders are in the background.

continued from page 97

When fed on the same ration scale, in mixed groups, gilts often grow faster than castrates, but castrates invariably tend to grade worse when slaughtered at the same liveweight. Castrates lay down fat more rapidly, and fat growth accelerates as the pig gets heavier. To achieve equal grading results with the gilts and castrates, the castrates should be sent for slaughter lighter than the gilts. Increased fatness in the castrate would follow from the daily rate of protein deposition being lower than for the gilt. Nutritionally speaking, the castrates ought to get a diet with a slightly lower protein content fed on a lower ration scale.

Precision

Accuracy in formulating diets and calculating the nutrient needs of pigs is rendered meaningless if the diet is not rationed with equal accuracy. The problems of a variable protein supply with possible commensurate losses in protein growth have been discussed in Chapter 3; resolution depends upon the unproven phenomenon of compensatory protein growth. However, a slight excess of dietary protein would help to ensure that maximum lean growth continues even if diet intake fluctuates. Again, an extension of the total fattening period caused by ration reduction would allow compensation for loss of lean growth in terms of the daily rate. Eight days' extension to a 100-day fattening period can result in an extra 4 kg of lean gain which is equivalent to 40 g daily over the fattening period.

Compensatory fat growth is less contentious. Pigs make up for a day's lost fat growth by extra growth later on when more energy comes available. The relevant difference between lean growth and fat growth is that lean growth is time-based—so much per day—whereas fat growth is dependent upon the amount of surplus energy available. This difference between lean growth and fat growth is fundamental to rationing. Where there may be no possibility of compensation, as with lean growth, then if the maximum daily lean gain is to be attained, the dietary needs for lean must be supplied on a daily basis, or potential growth will be irretrievably lost.

Maximum lean growth daily may not *always* be sought, in which case compensatory *lean* growth *is* feasible; where the daily maximum is 450 g lean but only 400 g average is required, then one day's growth of 350 g may be compensated by 450 g the next day.

With fat growth, there can be compensation so it is not necessary to supply the energy on a strict daily basis. Provided that the desired total amount of energy is supplied, its distribution is not crucial. The maximum rate of fat growth is not set by a time limit, but by the appetite limit for energy. So long as only fat growth is involved as a result of day to day fluctuations in diet supply, or where maximum lean growth is not required, the total weekly allowance of nutrients is more important than day-to-day exactitudes.

The need to ration carefully also depends upon the cost/unit weight of the diet and the penalties to be paid for over-fatness. Where the diet is cheap and the grade not of paramount importance, failure to ration carefully becomes correspondingly less important.

Pigs are usually fed in pens of 8–20 or more pigs. Competition creates between-pig differences in feed intakes, with consequential variation in growth rate and spread of the period over which pigs reach slaughter weight. There is much to be said in these circumstances for the time-based scale. Rationing by time also makes no judgments about the pigs as they grow, and therefore allows pigs to catch up by compensatory fat growth if they have suffered a growth check. Advocates for feeding by time rather than weight suggest that variation between pigs is reduced. It is regrettable that pigs cannot always also be sent to slaughter by time rather than by weight; considerable savings would be had in the use of pen space (allowing instant emptying) and in management. It is easier to clear fattening pens instantaneously when the pigs are destined for a market which accepts a range of slaughter weights (some pork and heavy trades, for example), rather than for the bacon market, for which the slaughter weight range is narrow.

PREGNANT SOWS

The large appetite of pregnant sows relative to their needs means that there is an opportunity to use ingredients of low nutrient density in pregnant sows diets. Thus, sows may be fed up to 4 or 5 kg of a low density diet to provide the same amount of energy and protein that would conventionally be provided by 2 kg daily of a cereal-based diet. For cereal-based diets the digestible energy (DE) value is usually between 12·5 and 13 MJ DE/kg diet and this density tends to be assumed when feed is rationed by weight. Thus, 2 kg provides about 25 MJ of DE.

Flat rate or scale?

As to the increasing foetal load as pregnancy progresses; with the increased efficiencies of pregnancy anabolism, the pig can probably take care of this herself. There is, therefore, little necessity to ration the feed to an increasing scale as the pregnancy progresses. A flat rate over the whole of pregnancy is acceptable.

The flat rate that is chosen should depend upon the size of the sow—that is, her maintenance requirement—and the desired rate of daily gain. As the animal ages and approaches maturity there is progressively less need for weight gains of maternal tissue. Conversely, as the animal ages it also gets larger and the maintenance demands rise. The daily maintenance requirement for a 120 kg gilt is about 18 MJ DE, whereas that for a mature sow of 200 kg is about 27 MJ DE, an increase of 50 per cent.

The need for weight gain

There is a straightforward need for a sow to gain weight in pregnancy. Were she not to do so, the products of conception might not suffer dramatically, but the maternal body would be depleted. Animals losing weight in pregnancy will enter lactation with low body stores of fat; lactation will itself be adversely affected, and reproductive capacity will be reduced with a likelihood of an increase in the delay between weaning and successful mating.

It is equally possible for sows to make excessive weight gain in pregnancy. The resulting obesity is likely to reduce embryo and foetal survival, and to being about problems at farrowing; particularly difficulties in the initiation of the lactation and clumsiness of the sow leading to piglet losses. In addition, the deposition of excess fat is, of itself, financially unrewarding: both in terms of food wastage and in terms of merely producing bigger sows which have higher maintenance requirements.

Amount of weight gain

The pregnancy ration is governed by the amount of weight gain required to be made over the course of the pregnancy. This will depend upon the amount of sow growth yet to be made (that is, how mature she is), the current state of fat reserves, and the condition of the sow. Condition in this context being the relationship between size and weight. There is a considerable variation in sow size at the same age. Thus, sows may be of equal weight and age, but because one is of larger size, she is more rangy and carries less fat.

The weight of individual piglets in the litter also appears to be related to the rate of weight gain in sows. The more food given to the sow in pregnancy, the heavier the pigs tend to be at birth. The relationship is shown in Figure 7.2. The solid line represents the average expectation, and the region lying between the two broken lines shows the possible range of responses as they might vary from farm to farm. Thus on one unit a ration of 2 kg may result in an average birth weight of just over 1 kg, whereas on another unit the same ration may produce piglets averaging 1·3 kg.

As Figure 7.2 shows, increasing the ration of pregnant sows is a means of increasing birth weight of piglets. The wisdom of such action will be considered again later, but it is already apparent from Figure 7.2, that a great deal of food requires to be given to the sow for relatively small increases to be gained in piglet birth weight.

It has been calculated previously that the pregnant sow, programmed to gain about 20 kg of maternal body in pregnancy, would usually need in the region of 210 g dietary crude protein daily and about 25 MJ DE, which corresponds quite closely to 2 kg of a diet of about 13 MJ DE/kg and 11 per cent crude protein. If maternal weight gain costs about 26 MJ of DE/kg, then 1 kg of weight gain may be achieved by an extra 2 kg of a standard cereal-based diet with 13 MJ DE/kg. This works out at about 0·2 kg diet daily over pregnancy for each 10 kg of sow weight change.

If 2 kg of diet with 13 MJ DE/kg and at least 11 per cent crude protein (9 per cent DCP) is taken as the standard for sows of about 140 kg being allowed some degree of maternal weight gain, then sows which require to make 10 kg less gain than the standard might be offered 1·8 kg daily and sows required to gain 10 kg more than the standard might be fed 2·2 kg. Table 7.2 gives some estimates of maternal body gain together with appropriate rations. Low gains appropriate for obese sows might be achieved by the 1·8 kg ration. Thin sows, however, may need to be fed liberally to gain 30–40 kg of maternal body.

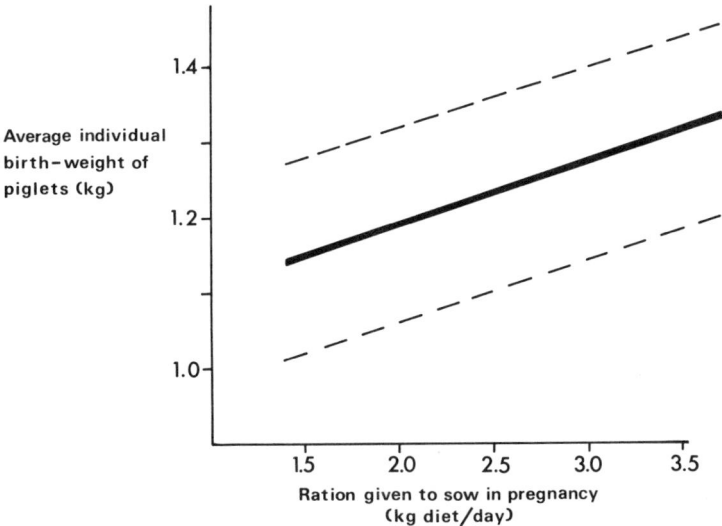

Figure 7.2. The effect of pregnancy ration upon the birth weight of piglets.

The expected requirements of DE given in Table 7.2 are only for purposes of guidance. The actual amounts needed will be different for sows of different liveweight and age and will also vary considerably from unit to unit. The 'standard' DE requirement for 20 kg of maternal gain may readily vary from 1·8 to 2·6 kg. Thus the same output in terms of maternal gain, litter size and piglet weight may be achieved with widely different daily rations during pregnancy. It is necessary for individual units to ascertain their own particular 'standard' level; and having produced their internal standard, the rationing regime needs to be scaled up or down accordingly.

TABLE 7.2. Weight gains (kg) in sows made in the course of pregnancy.

	Regime				
	Standard	Debilitating	Reducing	Replenishing	Fattening
Foetuses, membranes etc.	15-20	15-20	15-20	15-20	15-20
Maternal body	18-22	0	8-12	25-35	35-45
Total (approximate)	38	18	28	48	58
DE required[1]	26	21	23·5	28.5	31
Ration (kg of diet)[2]	2	1·6	1·8	2·2	2·4

[1]Calculated for a sow of about 140 kg liveweight.
[2]Assuming a diet of 13 MJ DE/kg. Lower density diets must be fed at proportionately higher rates. At 10 MJ DE/kg, for example, 2·6 kg are required to provide 26 MJ DE daily.

LACTATING SOWS

If the sow is offered feed *ad lib*, the amount of diet she will eat in lactation is inversely related to the amount that she was fed in pregnancy. But, on the other hand, sows fed liberally in pregnancy also have less need of food in lactation since they can make use of ample body stores.

If the sow has been fed adequately in pregnancy, but not excessively, she will contain sufficient fat to readily sustain a lactation weight loss of about 10 kg. Indeed, if the sow has a litter of nine or more piglets, some weight loss is almost inevitable because the nutrient needs for lactation exceed her appetite intake.

The lactation ration should make allowance for the next conception which, hopefully, will occur four days or so after the lactation is ended. If the sow is to conceive so soon after weaning, she must not come to the conclusion of her lactation in a nutritionally stressed and debilitated state.

The size of the litter sucking is a variable quantity. To control the rate of sow weight loss in lactation it is clearly necessary to ration according to the milk yield of the sow; that is, according to the number of piglets in the litter.

If a sow is under-fed in relation to her requirements, the yield of milk to the piglets will diminish and rapid body weight loss will occur. The effect of ration upon milk yield is particularly marked for large sows with high maintenance requirements and for lean sows with low fat reserves. Sows given inadequate nutrition in the first lactation can sustain milk yield from body reserves but in later lactation, the weight and leanness of sows becomes increasingly important.

In Table 7.3 are shown some rations for a diet of 15–16 per cent crude protein (13 per cent DCP) calculated for sows farrowing in average body condition.

In theory, sows which are larger, sows programmed to lose more or less than 10 kg in liveweight, or sows fatter or thinner than average, will need proportionately different quantities of feed. In practice, the ration scale should be sufficiently simple to be applicable to all lactating sows; allowance only being made for the number of piglets sucking—which is the major factor influencing the rate of energy use. From Table 7.3 it can be seen that the requirement for energy rises by about 5 MJ DE for each piglet suckled. This is equivalent to 0·4 kg of diet with 13 MJ DE/kg. An approximate rule of thumb for diets with 13 MJ DE/kg might be to give a ration of 4 kg for the sow and a litter of 5 piglets, and 0·4 kg for every piglet in the litter over 5. A sow with a litter of 10 would thus receive 6 kg daily.

The use of one ration, dependent only on the number of piglets in the litter, has the result that sows on the same feeding regime in lactation will lose weight at different rates. This failure to exactly provide for the dietary needs requires to be adjusted by means of the ration selected for the next pregnancy period. To achieve the readjustment necessary, the sows must be rationed as individuals in the pregnancy phase; if this is not allowed, there are likely to be adverse repercussions following from a failure to adequately control liveweight changes in the sow.

The final choice of ration will depend not only upon the energy density diet used, but also upon the individual circumstances of the unit. Because of differences in the strain of sow used, sows in some herds gain weight more slowly and have lower body weight. Again, some sows have smaller appetites than others, and therefore require a different pattern of feeding. The environment within which the sow is kept will also differ greatly between individual breeding units. In any event, it is probable that sows may need more or less than indicated in Table 7·3 to suckle the same number of piglets and to make the same weight losses.

TABLE 7.3. A rationing regime for lactating sows

Number of piglets in litter	Maintenance costs for sow of 140 kg (MJ DE/day)[1]	Energy needed for milk production (MJ DE/day)[2]	Dietary energy saved by breakdown of 10 kg of body fat tissue (MJ DE/day)[3]	Energy needed daily (MJ DE)	Ration (kg diet)[4]
5	21	44	11	54	4·2
6	21	48	11	58	4·5
7	21	53	11	63	4·8
8	21	58	11	68	5·2
9	21	62	11	72	5·5
10	21	67	11	77	5·9
11	21	72	11	82	6·3
12	21	76	11	86	6·6

[1] Assuming ME is 94 per cent DE, i.e. ME × 1·06 = DE
[2] 8·3 MJ ME or 8·8 MJ DE required/kg milk formed.
[3] 10 kg of fat lost over a 42 day lactation = 0·24 kg fat lost daily; if body yields up the equivalent of 44 MJ ME or 47 MJ DE per kg fat lost, then about 11 MJ of dietary DE is spared.
[4] Assuming the diet to contain 13 MJ DE/kg.

As was the case for rationing in pregnancy, it is necessary for each unit to adjust according to circumstance. The most simple test to assess the adequacy of the lactation ration is to weigh the sow to obtain some estimate of the rate of weight losses occurring. Figure 7.3 shows an example of the pattern of weight changes that can occur over the reproductive cycle. A different pattern of weight change can result in the same total gain over the cycle. This is because sows may gain less in pregnancy and lose less in lactation than has been shown in the figure, but still gain 15 kg from one weaning to the next. The total amount of gain made depends upon the total level of feed given over the reproductive cycle as a whole, but the distribution of feed between pregnancy and lactation controls the pattern of weight change during the course of each reproductive cycle.

Appetite

In addition to the restricted appetite of the lactating sow causing problems when large litters are sucking, her appetite is also depressed in the first few days following the stresses of parturition. The lactating sow is likely to benefit from being fed more than once daily. In addition, she should not be fed her full allowance immediately after farrowing, but only offered what will be readily cleared up within 20 minutes. In this way the sow can increase her intake at her own rate over the first week of lactation, up to the limit of her prescribed ration allowance.

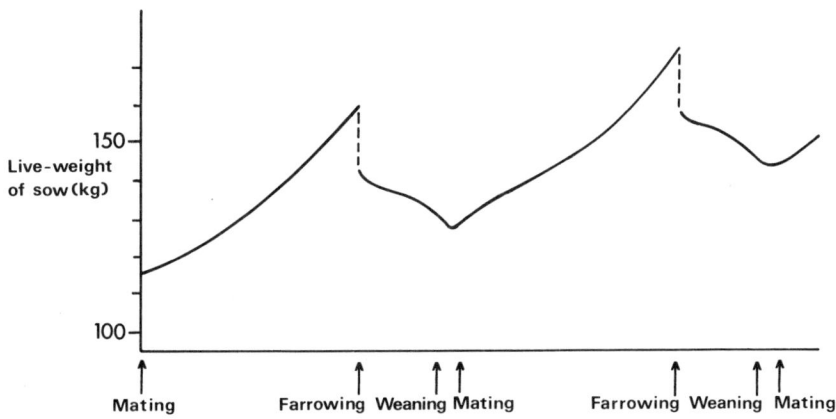

Figure 7.3. Example of weight changes during the reproductive cycle of sows.

WEANED SOWS FOR RE-BREEDING

The condition of the sow at the end of the reproductive cycle when her piglets are weaned is the result of the combination of pregnancy feeding, lactation feeding, milk yield and body condition. One reproductive cycle's end is the next cycle's beginning, and it is easy to understand how once a sow has become over-weight, she may get fatter and fatter as she progresses from cycle to cycle; or inversely, once she has become too lean and lacks the requisite body stores, she may get progressively thinner.

At weaning, the condition of the sow governs the stratagem to be used for her rationing until the next parturition. The first consideration, however, is to ensure that she will come into oestrus as soon as possible after weaning, and will conceive at first service.

Normally, sows will show oestrus four or five days after weaning. Allowing for some to return three weeks later, and others to be barren and fail to re-breed at all, the average time-lapse between weaning and conception over all the sows in a herd should be about twelve days.

Sows which have lactated for as little as two weeks or as long as eight weeks will usually be weaned in better condition than sows weaned at six weeks. In the first case, the lactation is of short duration and peak-yield is not yet reached; in the second case the peak of lactation has been passed, and unless the sow has a litter of 10 or more piglets it is likely that she will have already begun to replenish some of the body reserves lost three weeks earlier. The smaller the litter and the lower the lactation yield of the sow, the more likely is replenishment to take place. Sows suckling a large litter will, of course, continue to use body reserves for longer.

There are many differences of opinion concerning nutrition at the time of mating. Some consider that sows should be given ample feed up to and around the time of mating, other have failed to notice any nutritional effects at this time upon the ability of the sow to conceive. It is probable that much depends upon the condition of the sow concerned. Sows mated when too fat may have higher losses of embryos in early pregnancy. Sows that are too thin may either fail to show oestrus, or if mated, not conceive. The nutritional regime should be sufficiently generous for the sow to be in a rising or improving condition. Given these principles, and assuming the sow to be not obese at the end of lactation, a ration in the region of 2·6 kg (2·2 kg–3·0 kg) daily of a diet of 13 MJ DE/kg is appropriate.

INDIVIDUAL FEEDING OF SOWS

Rationing growing pigs assumes that the individual is amongst companions in a pen. The variations in pig intake and pig growth which result, prevent batch slaughter and make for management problems in the clearing of pens as the pigs come up to slaughter weight. However, it is generally accepted that the penalties incurred are less costly than the expenses that would follow from individual feeding arrangements for growing pigs.

In the case of sows, however, the penalties of group feeding are of greater practical importance. The body condition of the sow and the level of her fat reserves can only be controlled when each sow is rationed individually. Not only do sows vary intrinsically in their nutrient needs, but the different circumstances which befall sows as they age, require their individual treatment. When fed in groups, sows need to be carefully matched, because under group conditions sow weight changes can fluctuate wildly, and, in addition, thin sows tend to get thinner and fat sows fatter; precisely the opposite to the objectives of controlled feeding. The higher the density of stocking, the lower the level of feeding, and the greater the productivity of the unit, the more important it becomes to feed sows individually.

Chapter 8

CHOOSING A FEEDING PROGRAM FOR GROWING PIGS
— with the help of a model

IT IS a truism that the pig producer must react to change in order to remain profitable. The problem is, *how* should he react?

Management decisions can only be taken when the manager possesses objective information upon which to base his judgement. Nutritional decisions require fore-knowledge of what will befall an alteration in nutritional policy.

Responses of pigs to *static* circumstances may be forecast with historical information, but this is unworkable where circumstances are changing. To keep abreast of world feedstuff supplies, genetic improvements in stock, changes in overhead costs, and widely fluctuating market outlets, one thing a pig production system must *not* be is static.

An example can illustrate the problem. A producer is faced with a change in the terms of his bacon contract, such that the preferred weight at slaughter is increased by 5 kg, while the other details of the grading scheme remain the same. It is apparent that:
1. As the pigs are to be heavier at slaughter, they will be fatter. There will be an increase in the proportion of pigs in the lower grades.
2. Pigs will be in the pens for longer, so if the ration stays the same, fewer pigs will be sold in the year.
3. More feed will be eaten and feed efficiency will get worse.

Various courses of action are possible, and the responses made by different producers should vary—if the responses are to be correct.
1. Improve quality of stock so they grow faster and grade better.
2. Feed pigs less so they grow slower but leaner.
3. Feed pigs more to maintain throughput.
4. Improve the quality of the diet to ensure maximum lean meat growth.
5. Accept that the new contract is likely to reduce returns and trim back the system to cut costs.

6. Abandon the bacon contract and go for a different market outlet.

The service offered to the producer by the nutritionist has tended to be in the way of recommending generalised diet specifications and rationing regimes. Unfortunately, this type of information is more appropriate to stable production conditions and a high degree of standardisation in pigs and pig management systems. It is less useful where there is the degree of diversity that exists in the pig industry, and where the rigours of a changing environment must be met if the pig production system is to optimise financial returns. Any *single recipe* for success is likely to be wrong for many producers much of the time.

APPROACHES TO PREDICTING PIG RESPONSES

To react effectively to a change in circumstance, the producer should have some idea of the outcome of his actions *before* he takes them. If the historical approach to prediction is abandoned, two others remain: an on-farm experiment can be conducted under the new conditions, or the responses of pigs can be predicted by means of mathematical calculations which *simulate* numerically what the actual responses of live pigs would have been.

The on-farm trial approach has been advocated for some time, but it has some serious disadvantages. First, to be sure the right experiment is being done, a range of treatments are required, not just one. Secondly, experiments cost money. Lastly, *if* one gets a result, when one gets it—it may well be out of date.

Increasing interest is being shown by a number of groups in the simulation or model approach. There are many ways of tackling the construction of a pig simulator, and different groups use different methods. The modelling approach used at Edinburgh builds up the model pig from basic physiological principles.

Protein and fat growth of pigs are responses to the inputs of energy and protein from the diet, and so may be calculated by use of the same fundamental information described in earlier chapters. By this means, the daily gains of protein and lipid can be determined. Lean mass can be estimated as protein multiplied by about 4·5 (the factor changing with age) and fat mass as fat multiplied by 1·1. The other components of the live growth of the pig are the minerals (ash)—about 3 per cent of the liveweight; and the contents of the alimentary tract—about 5 per cent of liveweight.

What data there are suggest that the proportions of lean and fat in the carcase side may be approximated by multiplying the proportion of protein and fat in total body by 4·26 and 1·23 respectively, there

TABLE 8.1. Tentative relationship between model fat in carcase side and model P_2 measurement.[1]

Fat in carcase side (%)	P_2 (mm)
20	16·7
25	20·8
30	25·0
35	29·2
40	33·3
45	37·5

[1]Derived from the equation P_2 (mm) = 0·85 fat (%) − 0·83 at 100 kg.

TABLE 8.2. Guide to expected grades[1] from P_2 measurement of the model pig

P_2 measurement (mm)	Grade A	Percentage in Grade B	Grade C
18	76	23	1
20	50	42	8
22	32	45	23
24	21	38	41
26	12	20	68

[1]P_2 < 20 mm grade A; P_2 20-25 mm grade B; P_2 > 25 mm grade C

being a little more fat in the carcase side than in the offals. A difficult step to take is the link between percentage fat in the carcase and the thickness of fat along the back—the P_2 probe measurement which is instrumental in determining grade. However, approximations have been attempted and these are to be found in Table 8.1 (percentage fat to P_2) and Table 8.2 (P_2 to grade).

Unquestionably, this sort of calculation is prone to error. From the original inputs of dietary DE and DCP estimates are made step by step in simulation of the actual physiological events in the pig, until finally the grade is predicted. Error can arise both in the data used at each step and in the logic concerning nutrient use.

No apology is made for the Edinburgh model. It is justified on three counts:

1. The calculated predictions are close to results from live pig experiments.
2. Alternative ways of predicting response are generally unacceptable and/or equally prone to error.
3. The model is flexible and can incorporate a range of nutritional and other conditions which are likely to vary between producers.

CHOOSING A FEEDING PROGRAM FOR GROWING PIGS

The way the calculation is made

The physiological information is incorporated into a series of linked equations which are formed into a computer program. Although the logic is simple, as has been shown at the end of Chapters 3 and 4; for accurate, rather than approximate, results the mathematics become too complex for hand calculations. The model pig takes in the nutrients it is fed, and grows accordingly day by day. One day's results are added to the next until the prescribed slaughter weight (or age) is reached. All the information about the growth process and the characteristics of the final product (model bacon) is printed out and can be simply read off. The computer takes about two minutes or so to complete the iterative and integrating processes that simulate six months of a pig's life.

As it stands at the moment, the Edinburgh model allows for differences in—and therefore needs specific information about—

1. Pig type, as indicated in Table 2.3; expressed in terms of the maximum rate at which protein can be deposited in growth (abbreviated to max PD).
2. Ration; daily.
3. Diet specification; digestible energy (DE), digestible crude protein (DCP) and biological value of the protein (BV).
4. Start weight and slaughter weight (or age).
5. Temperature of the environment.

The Edinburgh model does not yet allow for a number of factors which are important, but to date have not been adequately quantified.

6. General level of management.
7. Disease status.
8. Moving and mixing of pigs.

Lastly, some items are not considered, because although they might impinge upon the general level of performance on a unit, they do not interact with the pig's responses to changes made in factors 1 to 5 above. These items would include, for example: feeding method, wet/dry, meal/pellets, once/twice daily, protein feed separated from cereal feed, irregular feeding intervals, floor/trough and so on.

Average responses

If a range of assumptions are made about average conditions, then the response to just a single change in a variable can be examined. These are given in Table 8.3. Being general, this information is of limited use, but does give a quick guide to the magnitude and direction of the responses which can be expected to the changes listed.

TABLE 8.3. Approximations of expected changes in growth and fatness

	Average growth rate (g/day)	Carcase quality by P_2 probe (mm backfat)
Ration: + 0·1 kg diet daily	+50	+1·5
Weight at slaughter: + 1·0 kg weight at slaughter	+ 5	+0·5
Energy density of diet: +1·0 MJ DE/kg diet	+50	+1·5
Protein in diet: +1% (10g/kg) DCP in diet		
up to 130 g/kg	+20	—0·8
above 130 g/kg	—10	—0·5
Strain of pig: + 10 g protein deposition in growth daily	+30	—2·0

RESPONSES PARTICULAR TO INDIVIDUAL CIRCUMSTANCES

The main shortcomings of the data in Table 8.3 are immediately apparent. One is given no information about what happens if more than one change is made. For example, how an increase in protein content of the diet might influence live gain over a range of different energy densities. Further, the table assumes that the responses are linear; that there will be the same response to the next increment as to the first. This is not likely to be true.

All individual circumstances cannot be presented on the printed page. In addition, for purposes of example, it is best that only two or three production factors are altered at one time. Solutions to particular problems are best obtained from the model direct; in this way all the various factors involved can be set up appropriate to individual circumstances. However, situations can be presented which serve to exemplify the objectives and possibilities of the model approach to response prediction.

EXAMPLE 1 (Figure 8.1):
How do pigs respond to a change in level of feeding (ration scale)? How does strain of pig (genotype), or sex, influence the response?

To answer these questions the model pig has been set up to consume a diet of 13 MJ DE and 150 g DCP/kg. The biological value of the protein was 70 and the temperature of the house 18°C. The pig is started off at 20 kg liveweight and the computer instructed to grow it until 100 kg liveweight is reached. These details are given at the bottom of the figure. Three types of pig were chosen to represent three strains: poor, average and good. The same types can also represent castrates, gilts and boars, in that order. The type deter-

CHOOSING A FEEDING PROGRAM FOR GROWING PIGS

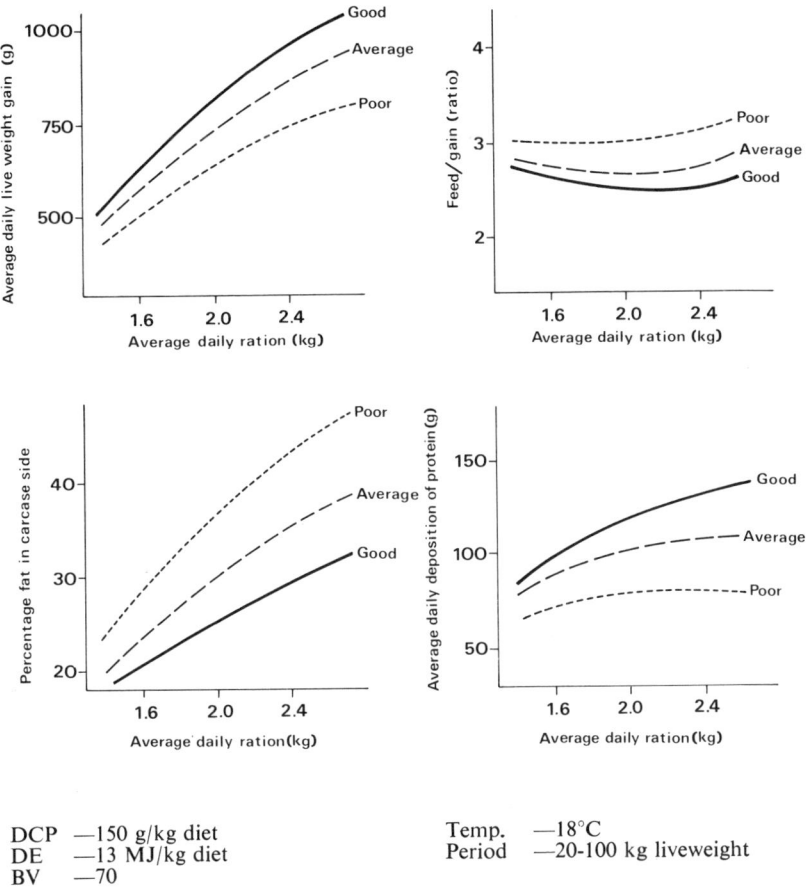

DCP —150 g/kg diet
DE —13 MJ/kg diet
BV —70

Temp. —18°C
Period —20-100 kg liveweight

Figure 8.1. Responses to level of feeding (ration scale) by growing pigs with three different maximum limits to their daily rate of protein deposition:
Poor = 80 g protein deposition/day (Max PD- 80)
Average = 110 g protein deposition/day (Max PD-110)
Good = 140 g protein deposition/day (Max PD-140)

mines the maximum protein growth (max PD) that the pig could make (see Table 2.3), and three maximum rates were chosen; 80 g, 110 g, and 140 g of protein deposited daily. Lastly, each type of pig is fed on a variety of ration scales so that the relationship between pig type and feeding scale can be examined. Results are obtained for average daily gain over the growth period, average feed conversion ratio (feed/liveweight gain), percentage of fat in the carcase (which dictates grade), and average daily rate of protein deposition. These results have been graphed out and are given in Figure 8.1.

An average daily ration of 1·6 kg is achieved on a scale which starts at 0·8 kg diet when the pig weighs 20 kg and increases smoothly in the manner of ration scale D of Figure 7.1 to reach 2·5 kg when the pig weighs 100 kg. An average ration of 2·0 kg is achieved by scale which starts at 0·95 kg at 20 kg liveweight, and goes up to 3·2 kg at 100 kg liveweight. The scale for an average ration of 2·4 starts at 1·1 kg and goes up to 3·8 kg.

As the feed intake increases there is a dramatic increase in liveweight gain. Feed conversion ratio gets better and then gets worse (see also Figure 4.4). But it is apparent that conversion ratio is not all that greatly influenced by feeding level. Increasing the level of feeding makes the pig much fatter at slaughter, (with commensurate reduction in the standard of grading achieved), even though the rate of protein deposition tends to improve.

Conversely, leanness increases as food supply diminishes. In addition to reducing the amount of fat growth, slower growth increases leanness in another way. As the deposition of protein in the body of the pig is time based—so much per day—then the older the pig is at slaughter the more days have passed, each of which has led to the accumulation of another increment of protein. The greater the number of days to slaughter, the more lean must be in the carcase.

At all levels of intake the poor type of pig grows slower, has a worse conversion ratio and is fatter. The poor type maximises its average daily rate of protein deposition at an average daily ration of 2·0 kg, whereas the good type of pig goes on responding until an average daily intake of 2·6 kg or so in reached.

The good type of pig responds to increased feeding level by growing more lean, whereas the poor type responds by growing more fat. At an equal level of fatness of 30 per cent, good pigs can be fed a scale with an average of 2·5 kg, whereas poor pigs have to be restricted back to a scale with an average of 1·65 kg. At an intake of 1·65 kg the poor pig grows 530 g daily; at 2·5 kg the good pig grows 980 g daily. Only by means of reducing growth in this way can both pigs grade equally.

The ration scales used in Figure 8.1 are weight-based. A simple time-based scale was designed for purposes of comparison. The time scale was for 1·0 kg diet at 20 kg, increasing daily by 0·025 kg (0·75 kg each month). The model pig was set up to correspond to the average type in Figure 8.1. The pig on the time-based scale ate an average of 2·24 kg diet daily and grew from 20–100 kg in 100 days. If the 2·24 mark is found on the horizontal axis of the graphs in Figure 8.1, the performance of the average pig fed on the weight-based scale can be read off and compared to the performance of the same pig fed the time-based scale. Use of the time-based scale gave very similar results to the weight-based scale: 807 g daily liveweight gain, 2·7 feed conversion ratio, 33 per cent fat in carcase side, 107 g protein deposition daily.

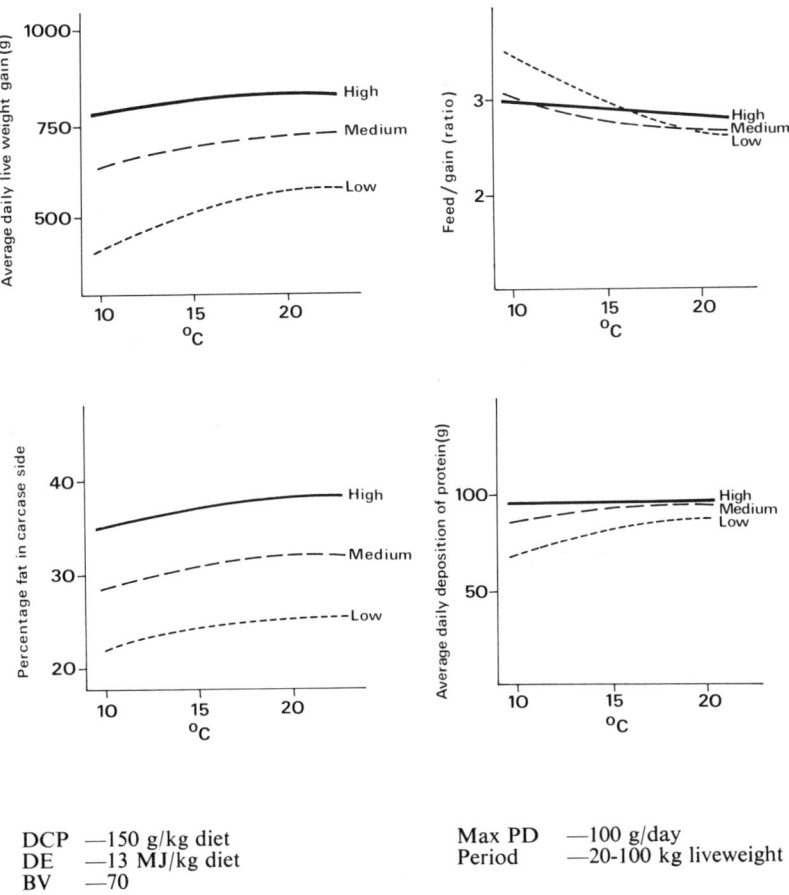

DCP —150 g/kg diet
DE —13 MJ/kg diet
BV —70

Max PD —100 g/day
Period —20-100 kg liveweight

Figure 8.2. Responses to house temperature by growing pigs given three ration scales:

	Low	Medium	High
Ration (kg) at 20 kg	0·80	0·95	1·1
Ration (kg) at 100 kg	2·5	3·2	3·8
Average daily	1·6	2·0	2·4

EXAMPLE 2 (Figure 8.2):

What are the effects of environmental temperature in relation to the level of feeding?

Details for setting up the model are laid out in Figure 8.2 (p.117) in the same way as described for Figure 8.1. In this case the effect of house temperature is studied with pigs given three ration scales; high, medium and low. A fall in temperature to about 12°C has little

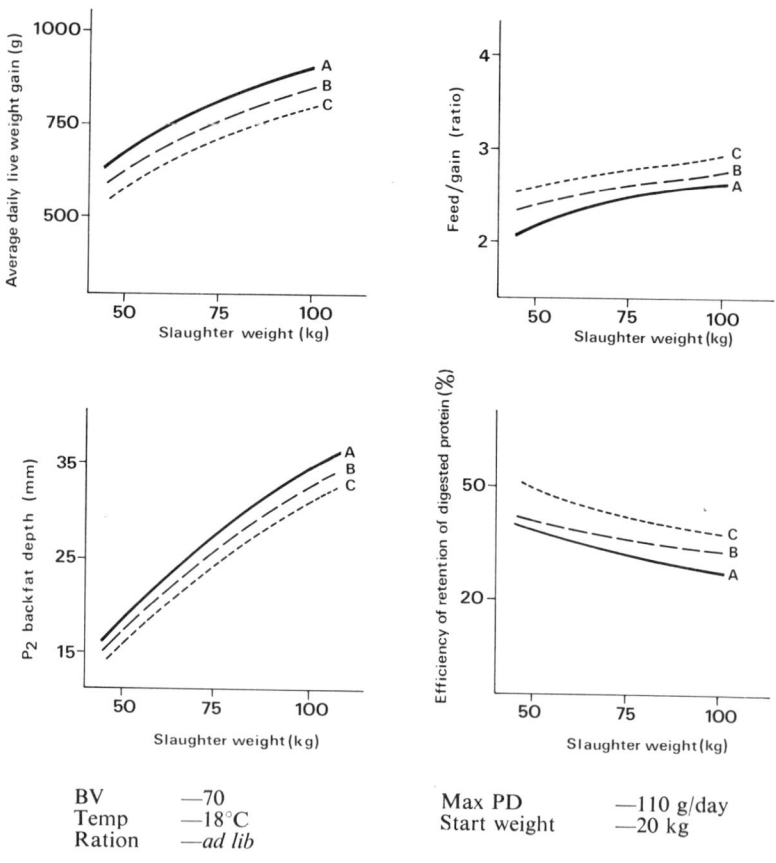

BV	—70	Max PD	—110 g/day
Temp	—18°C	Start weight	—20 kg
Ration	—ad lib		

Figure 8.3. Responses of growing pigs according to weight at slaughter and diet:
Diet A = 14 MJ DE and 170 g DCP/kg diet
Diet B = 13 MJ DE and 145 g DCP/kg diet
Diet C = 12 MJ DE and 120 g DCP/kg diet

effect upon pigs fed liberally. These pigs are growing faster, giving off more heat, and are thereby more resistant to cold. The pigs on the low feeding level grow much slower and are more affected by a drop in temperature. From 20°C, each further fall in temperature reduces the rate of gain and worsens the feed conversion ratio. At the medium level of feeding a fall in temperature from 20–10°C reduces gain by 85 g daily or about 12 per cent.

EXAMPLE 3 (Figure 8.3):
How does a change in slaughter weight influence grade and average performance? Is this much affected by the nutrient density of the diet?

The model pig is offered three diets *ad lib* – A, B, or C, representing high nutrient density, medium and low density diets of different energy: protein ratios *(see Figure caption)*. The pigs are slaughtered over the weight range 50 to 100 kg. As pigs are kept to heavier weights they grow faster, convert food and protein less efficiently and get considerably fatter.

In general, the effect of diet density is relatively small. The high density diet (A) results in the best performance for gain and feed efficiency, but the carcases are fatter. At equal intakes the pig fed the lower density diet grows slower and has the leaner carcase. For equal backfat thickness, the slower growing pig can be taken to a heavier weight. At equal slaughter weight, the pig fed the lower density diet has less backfat. It is clear that if a slaughter weight of 90–95 kg is selected, for the P_2 measurement to be reduced below 25 mm, some form of feed restriction is necessary. The ration scale would need to be most severe for diet (A).

EXAMPLE 4 (Figures 8.4, 8.5 and 8.6):
What benefits can result from increasing the protein content of the diet? How does protein quality interact with protein content? Do different pig types react differently to different levels of DCP in the diet? Does the energy level of the diet influence a pig's response to protein? Should a change in diet protein content be accompanied by a change in diet energy content?

Raising the protein level of the diet improves daily liveweight gain up to a peak, after which rate of gain decreases (Figure 8·4). The pigs become less fat, and although the rate at which fatness is reduced tails off at the higher levels of dietary protein, the response continues beyond the point at which daily gain has peaked. At the higher levels of dietary protein, growth is slower and this makes for leanness. Further, progressively more of the energy in the diet (which remained

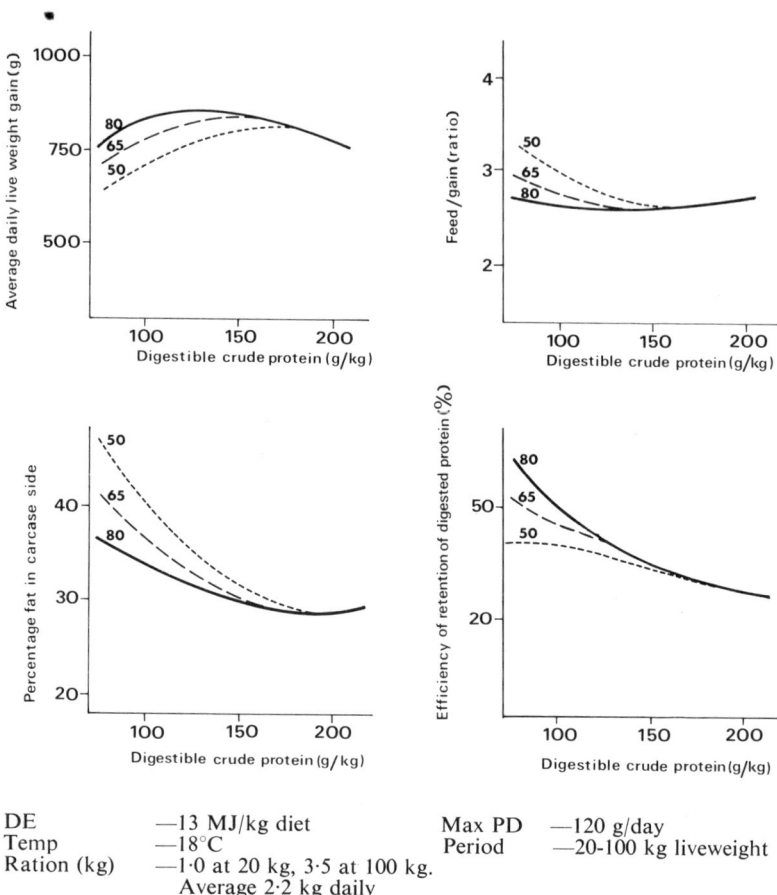

DE	—13 MJ/kg diet	Max PD	—120 g/day
Temp	—18°C	Period	—20-100 kg liveweight
Ration (kg)	—1·0 at 20 kg, 3·5 at 100 kg.		
	Average 2·2 kg daily		

Figure 8.4. Responses of growing pigs to concentration of dietary protein of three biological values:

$BV=50$ $BV=65$ $BV=80$

fixed at 13 MJ DE/kg) is contained in the protein fraction, and because of the energy used for deamination the actual energy realised is less than the dietary DE suggests. The effective reduction in energy intake reduces gain and lowers fat in the carcase. To improve carcase grade by excessive levels of diet protein is, however, rather expensive; giving less feed would have a similar result (Figure 8.1).

Biological values of 50, 65 and 80 represent three levels of protein quality, at levels above 170 g DCP/kg diet, responses to protein

CHOOSING A FEEDING PROGRAM FOR GROWING PIGS

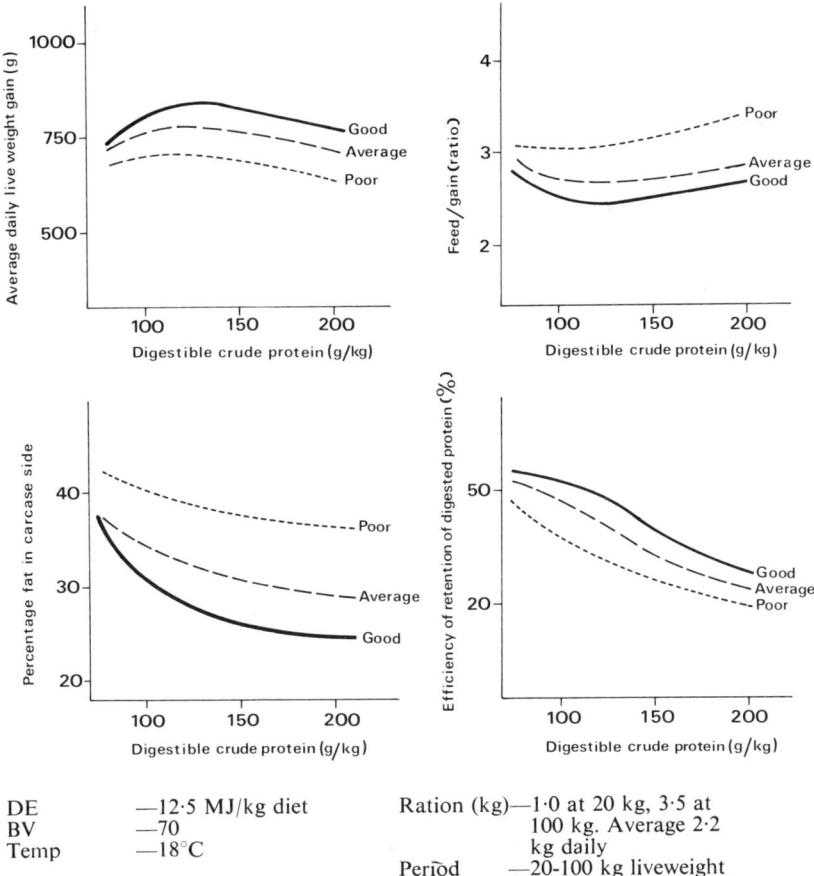

DE	—12·5 MJ/kg diet
BV	—70
Temp	—18°C

Ration (kg)—1·0 at 20 kg, 3·5 at 100 kg. Average 2·2 kg daily
Period —20-100 kg liveweight

Fig. 8.5. Responses to concentration of dietary protein by growing pigs with different maximum limits to their daily rate of protein deposition (lean growth):

Poor   = Max PD- 80
Average = Max PD-110
Good   = Max PD-140

quality merge and there are no differences. At progressively lower dietary concentrations of DCP, the higher quality protein (BV 80) brings about the best results for all the characteristics measured. This is because pigs offered DCP of lower quality (BV 65, BV 50) run into a deficit of balanced essential amino acids, cannot maximise their lean growth, and grow fat.

Daily liveweight gains of 800 g can be achieved on a diet with 9 per cent DCP (about 11 per cent CP) at BV 80, 12 per cent DCP (about 15 per cent CP) at BV 65 and 16 per cent DCP (about 20 per cent CP) at BV 50. Digested protein is, of course, more efficiently retained when the BV is higher. Efficiency of retention also improves as the level of dietary protein is reduced.

The responses of pigs with maximum rates of protein deposition (max PD) of 80 g, 110 g and 140 g are drawn up in Figure 8.5. For daily gain the humped-back response curve is again shown. This is mirrored in the feed/gain ratio; faster growing pigs having the better conversion efficiency, both within one pig type and when good and poor pig types are compared. Good pigs respond faster and for longer to increasing dietary levels of protein. Thus the slope of the responses in gain, efficiency and fatness are steeper for good pigs, and the levels of production higher (for gain and efficiency) or lower (for fatness).

The peak of response in daily liveweight gain for good pigs is at about 13 per cent DCP (approximately 16 per cent CP); the peak for poor pigs is at about 11 per cent DCP. For carcase quality, most of the rapid improvement by good pigs is again to be had up to 13 per cent DCP. Poor pigs have a less dramatic improvement in carcase leanness with increasing dietary protein than do good pigs.

To grow protein (lean), pigs need energy as well as protein. For an increase in daily protein deposition to occur, more energy must be available for the extra protein deposition. Responses to supplements of dietary protein might be expected therefore to continue to a higher level in the presence of ample energy.

Figure 8.6 shows two of the pig types already looked at in Figure 8.5; poor, with 80 g/day maximum protein deposition (max PD), and good, with 140 g/day max PD. These pig types are offered diets with 80–200 g DCP/kg (as in Figure 8.5), but this time also with two levels of dietary energy concentration: 12·5 and 14·0 MJ DE/kg.

For the poor pig (80 g/day, max PD), an increase in energy density raises the general level of performance, but there is no evidence that the response to increasing diet protein continues to a higher level for the diet with the greater energy concentration. That is, the peak in response occurs at similar levels of DCP for both levels of DE. In the case of the good pigs, however, not only is the performance better on the diet with 14 MJ DE/kg, but the peak in response to DCP *does* occur at a higher dietary protein level (14 per cent DCP). The model pig therefore suggests that the influence of the energy density of the diet upon the pig's response to increasing levels of dietary protein is relatively small, and only likely to be of practical importance for the better strains of pigs.

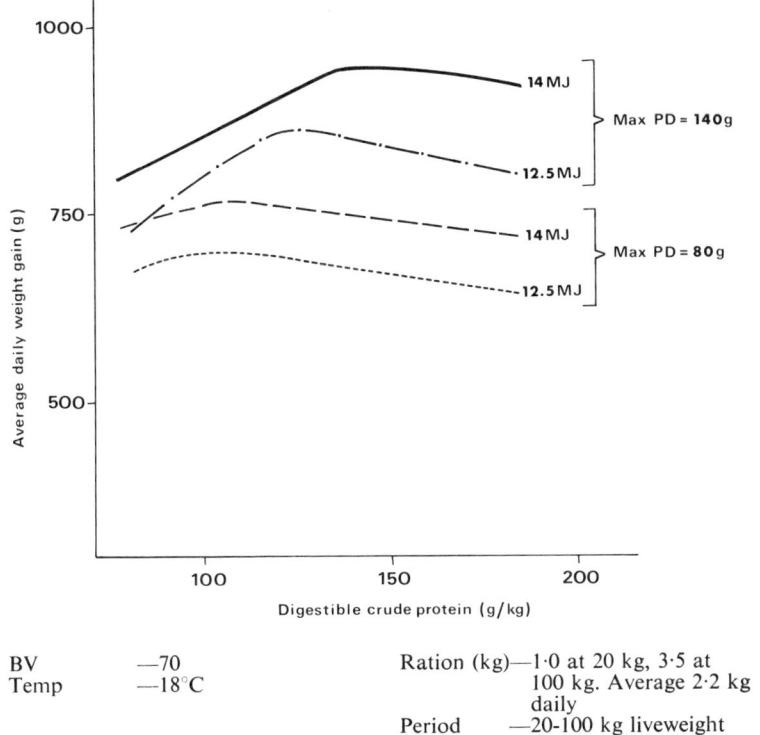

Figure 8.6. Responses to concentration of dietary protein in diets with different energy densities by growing pigs with different maximum limits to their daily rate of protein deposition (lean growth):

14 MJ DE/kg diet
12·5 MJ DE/kg diet } Maximum protein in deposition 140 g daily
14 MJ DE/kg diet
12·5 MJ DE/kg diet } Maximum protein deposition 80 g daily

General level of performance of the model pig

For purposes of demonstration, the standards chosen for both diets and pigs have been quite high, with the result that performances by the model have tended to be rather better than would be found in some practical situations. In order to show that this is caused by the values used in setting up the model, and not by some quality of the model itself, a final run was set up to examine what would happen to the model pig under more spartan conditions. The model was fed a ration scale which reached 2·5 kg (5·5 lb) at 100 kg liveweight, of a diet with 12 MJ DE/kg and 100 g DCP/kg (BV 60, about 13 per cent

CP). The strain of pig was identified by a max PD of 70 g daily, and the house temperature was set at 8°C. The model pig grew at 361 g/day, taking 222 days to grow from 20–100 kg. The feed/gain ratio was 4·2. As a carcase, the pig was quite acceptable because it grew so slowly—having a P_2 measurement of 19·7 mm and 24·2 per cent fat in the carcase side.

USE OF RESULTS FOR FINANCIAL CALCULATIONS

Ultimately, pig nutrition is a financial exercise, but useful financial calculations have been held up largely as a result of a shortage of biological information. The model helps to surmount this hurdle by enabling prediction of the outcome of changes in nutritional policy. Armed with the biological information that the model yields, monetary values can be attributed to inputs and outputs, and the financial outcome of the biological prediction can be derived.

Firstly, the inputs are scrutinised to provide for growth at least-cost; manipulations are made with feedstuffs of different prices, diets with different densities, proteins with different qualities, pigs of different type, houses with different environments and so on. Next, outputs are examined to maximise returns; different slaughter weights, various carcase qualities, a range of rates of growth and of feed efficiencies. Lastly, these two elements of the production process need to be simultaneously compared; the value of all the various combinations of the elements of output from the pig unit must be judged in relation to the costs of all the various combinations of inputs. It is then a husbandry and management exercise to implement the optimum program.

USE OF THE MODEL TO PRODUCE TARGETS AND IN DIAGNOSIS

The performance levels of the model pig and the responses it makes can serve to define target performance levels appropriate to the circumstances of individual units. Clearly, it is unrealistic to produce the same target performance levels for all pig producers to aim at. Level of biological performance is constrained by aspects of individual units which often cannot be, nor should be, changed.

The model can also help in diagnosing problems. The extent to which actual performance falls short of model pig performance gives a guide to the amount of production lost through inefficiencies of one sort or another.

Again, an estimation can be made of the contribution of various aspects or production to a particular problem situation. The extent to which housing may be blamed for poor performance can relate to level of feeding; the effects of low diet protein are likely to be less if the strain of pig is poor, and so on. Given some information about a unit, particular problems areas could be highlighted by adjusting the model to replicate the unit and to match existing performance figures. For example, it is possible by this means to pin-point a possible inadequacy of diet or ration.

Chapter 9

CHOOSING A FEEDING PROGRAM FOR THE BREEDING HERD

THE SELECTION of a feeding program for breeding stock is influenced by:
1. The need to safeguard continued productivity by breeding animals.
2. The desirability of achieving an acceptable level of productivity at the most cost effective level of feed input.

These objectives can be antagonistic to each other since the first objective suggests a need for a degree of 'insurance', while the second appears to demand that the safety margins are cut to the minimum.

It is possible to devise feeding systems which allow both objectives to be satisfied by the definition of minimum and maximum standards of intake. These limits should be selected so that at one extreme reproductive failures of nutritional origin are eliminated, and at the other, excessive intakes avoided. Having devised the limits between which there is freedom of choice, the most appropriate level can be chosen on the basis of the biological responses of the sow to changes in the feeding system. Maximum and minimum limits for energy and protein over the breeding cycle of sows are shown in Figures 9.1 and 9.2.

The 'appropriate' level will be selected after consideration has been given to:

(a) The price that the producer is willing to pay to ensure continued reproductive productivity;
(b) The reproductive performance that is considered adequate by individual producers;
(c) The features of the individual unit which demand certain constraints on management practices. (For example, the individual feeding facilities.)

In the case of minerals, vitamins and to a large extent in the protein quality aspects of the diet, the cost of inclusion of these components does not represent a high cost in relation to the potential benefits of an insurance factor. The risk of reproductive failure arising from a deficiency of a vitamin usually results in the inclusion of specified vitamins as listed in Table 5.3. Generalised recommendations which cover a wide range of environmental conditions will result in excess levels of vitamins and minerals and an over-supply of some amino acids under normal situations. The cost of this policy is cheerfully borne by most pig producers.

With regard to energy and total protein, and hence to feed intake, the position is very different. These nutrients comprise the major cost of producing weaned pigs, and the application of generalised feeding regimes will inevitably lead to a considerable and quite unwarranted financial burden on individual farms.

FACTORS AFFECTING CHOICE OF FEEDING LEVEL

The selection of the appropriate level within the maximum and minimum levels described in Figures 9.1 and 9.2 poses a range of

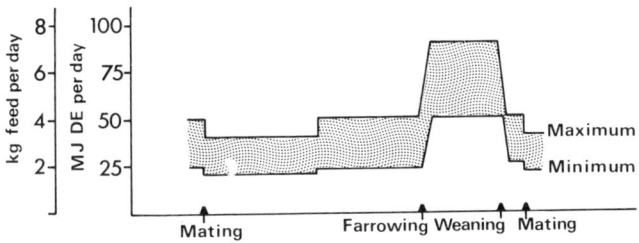

Figure 9.1. Maximum and minimum levels of energy intakes by sow. The area between the two levels represents the range of choice available.

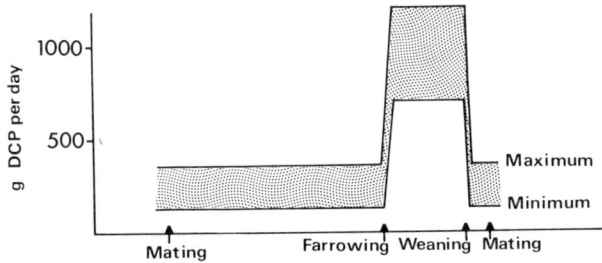

Figure 9.2. Maximum and minimum levels for digestible crude protein intakes by sows. The area between the two levels represents the range of choice available.

problems, and a variety of factors have to be taken into account. Some of these are related to the environment in which the sows are placed, some relate to the stage in the breeding cycle and some are due to individual characteristics of the sow; in particular, the liveweight and body condition.

Environment

The environment in which sows are maintained varies considerably; in ambient temperature, the presence or absence of draughts, the provision of bedding material, the behaviour of sows and the disease challenge which sows encounter.

Low temperatures influence productivity, particularly in relation to the liveweight changes of the sows. However, effects of house temperature will be mitigated by close contact between sows and the provision of a bed of straw or other material. The tethering of sows either in pregnancy or in lactation prevents bodily contact and bed-making, and although there may be few disadvantages when the sows are kept in favourable environments, in cold and draughty conditions the adverse effects of tethering individual sows upon performance can be substantial.

An additional important feature of the environment is the effect upon the sows of a bacterial or viral infection, or an infestation of intestinal worms or external parasites such as lice. These disease burdens are difficult to quantify in nutritional terms, but they represent important influences on the utilisation of the feed. For example, comparisons of the liveweight increases made by sows in herds both before and after the elimination of virus infection, by means of the minimal disease program, demonstrate that the difference between the two disease situations could be equivalent to 6 MJ DE/day (0·5 kg feed). The difficulty of establishing the disease pattern within a herd, and of adjusting the nutritional regime to take account of the presence of sub-clinical diseases, should not disguise the fact that under commercial conditions such adjustments are of considerable importance.

For sows maintained on pasture, an important aspect of their environment is the evaluation of the nutritive value of the grazing. Grassland can supply the equivalent of 13 MJ DE/day (1 kg feed) and all the protein needs of the pregnant sow, but only for the most productive season of the year. In winter conditions where the sow may be exposed to low temperature and rainfall, and during which the nutritive value of the forage is reduced, the extra energy involved in maintaining body temperature while the sow is grazing can more than outweigh the nutritive benefits of the forage ingested.

Individuality of sows

The most striking characteristic of sows is their variability in liveweight and body condition. A sow's liveweight is the result of a combination of factors such as the initial mating weight, the history of disease, the influence of management practices such as group housing, level of milk production, and the length of the interval between weaning and conception. There is also the physiological age of the sow as measured by her liveweight relative to her final mature body weight. These factors can result in sows weighing either 100 kg or 250 kg, even though attempts have been made to supply all sows in the unit with the same feed intake.

The feeding program must have as an objective either the reduction in variations in body weight of the sows or the development of a system which takes into account the differences in liveweight by a rationing scheme for individual sows. To ignore the range of bodyweights will inevitably mean that the feeding system selected for a particular unit only suits a small proportion of the herd.

Sows which are housed and fed in groups compete with each other for the available feed, and under most commercial situations sows are fed at levels below appetite for the major proportion of their breeding life. Under these circumstances, their feeding behaviour is of considerable importance. Thus the feed intake of sows in multiple-suckling systems relates to the number of sows in the pen despite feed being supplied in a feed hopper *ad lib*. This apparent contradiction is due to the dominance of some sows in defending the feed hopper during the periods when they are not themselves feeding. In pregnancy, when the feed intake may be only 30 per cent of appetite levels, even a generous allocation of trough space or the provision of a number of feeding sites fails to eliminate the inequality of the feed intake of individual sows, which may vary by up to 50 per cent. This could result in individual sows receiving intakes of feed which lie outside the limits suggested in Figure 9.1.

It is suggested that sows which are fed in groups should be given feed allowances which are about 15 per cent above that of sows fed individually, to ensure that those sows which are dominated by others receive feed intakes sufficient to preclude reproductive failure.

DISTRIBUTION OF FEED IN PREGNANCY AND LACTATION

In practice, it is unlikely that feed can be allocated so that it exactly meets the nutrient demand over the different phases of reproduction. It is fortunate that short-term discrepancies between supply and demand do not lead to disasters such as abortion or cessation of milk production.

The system which allocates sows a constant daily intake throughout the course of pregnancy obviously fails to allow for the changing needs of the sow. Although some feeding programs make a particular feature of increasing feed intake as pregnancy proceeds, this appears to be an unwarranted complexity. The changes in protein requirements as pregnancy proceeds are counter-balanced by the increased efficiency of protein utilisation which occurs in the course of the pregnancy. This means that the total protein available for metabolism increases in a similar way to the demand of the foetuses. In respect to energy intake, the changing demand during pregnancy is buffered by the mobilisation of fat reserves in the latter half of the pregnancy period. As long as the feed intake in any phase of pregnancy does not fall outside the limits shown in Figures 9.1 and 9.2, the distribution of feed within the pregnancy period does not appear to be of major importance provided only that the total feed required is ingested over the course of the pregnancy.

During lactation, the changes in daily milk production are small, although energy production in milk is lower for weeks 1 and 2 and weeks 7 and 8. These differences do not appear to be of sufficient magnitude to justify attempts to match the nutrient supply to the small changes in energy demand which are caused by the changes in milk production which occur as the lactation progresses.

More controversial is the distribution of feed between pregnancy and lactation. In some instances there are advantages in allowing high intakes at one stage and a reduction in feed intake at a later stage; for example, the exploitation of seasonal production of grass. Another reason for distributing feed so that it does not correspond with daily demands arises where the sows are individually fed for a portion of the reproductive cycle; a higher overall feed intake is accepted during the group feeding phase with lower feed intakes during the period in which the sows are individually fed. Lastly, there are those who specifically advocate either high/low or low/high systems in pregnancy/lactation. Within the limits of feed intake indicated in Figure 9.1, there appears to be surprisingly little benefit from adopting either or neither of these systems.

The explanation of this somewhat surprising conclusion is that surplus energy consumed by the sow is deposited as fat which can then be subsequently mobilised for production purposes in times of energy shortage. Such deposition occurs more easily in pregnancy and fat mobilisation occurs readily in lactation. Deposition/mobilisation cycles are theoretically inefficient since each phase requires energy to effect the chemical changes involved. This inefficiency is only demonstrable in practice where body fat is mobilised for purposes of maintenance or for protein synthesis, since the energy costs of these transference processes are high. Normally, body fat is not mobilised for these purposes, adequate being provided in the daily dietary supply to specifiically avoid such inefficiencies (Figures 9.1 and 9.2). However, for the mobilisation of body lipid for milk synthesis, as is the more usual possibility, there is little inefficiency (as has been calculated in Chapter 4). In practical terms, it is the total intake of feed in the complete reproductive cycle that is crucial, and the distribution of feed between pregnancy and lactation is of less importance.

Records

The basis for the choice of a feeding regime for a particular unit will largely depend on the records which are available from that unit. If no performance data are available, the farmer will normally opt for a feeding regime which represents an average of the intakes shown in Figure 9.1 and 9.2. It is, however, difficult to justify such a lack of information, as breeding records are required for so many managerial decisions.

On most units information will be available for the main performance traits such as number of pigs born and frequency of farrowing, and an estimate can be made of the total feed intake in pregnancy and lactation. The choice of an optimum feeding program requires that this information be available.

The vital importance of this information stems from it being produced on the very unit for which the feeding program is being designed. In this respect it is more valuable than any data produced by research workers or farmers on other units. The individual farm data represent the unique effects of the interactions between the genetic potential of the pigs and the environment in which they are placed. Thus if poor buildings are available or sows are suffering from virus pneumonia, the required adjustments must be made to the feed intake. There is no way in which national standards can take into account these circumstances.

There is some virtue, however, in comparing feed intake and performance records from one unit with the comparable national data, since this helps to indicate the features of the farm which differ from the expected average. In comparisons of this type the sole use of performance data can be misleading, and the feed costs per unit of productivity is usually a more useful type of value to compare.

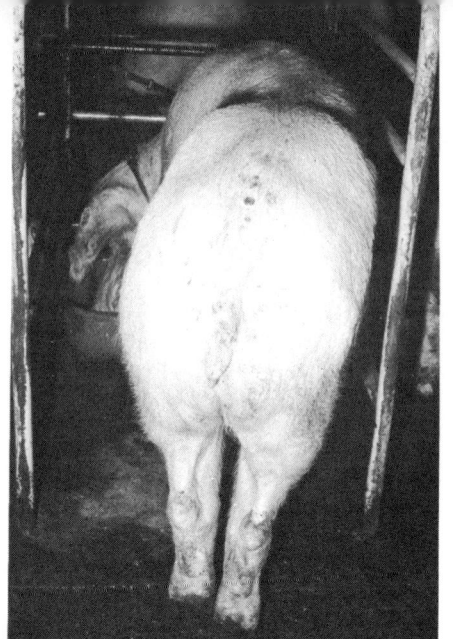

SOW CONDITION IN LATE PREGNANCY

10. Too thin.

11. About right.

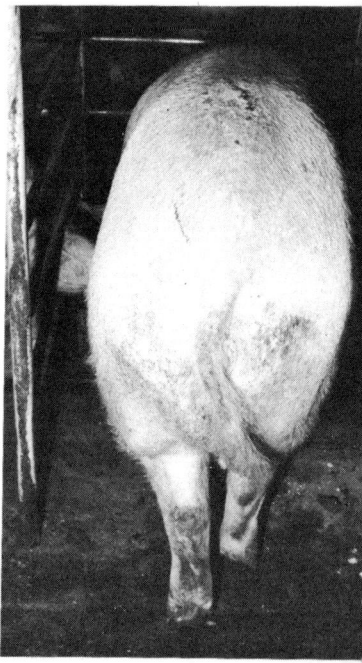

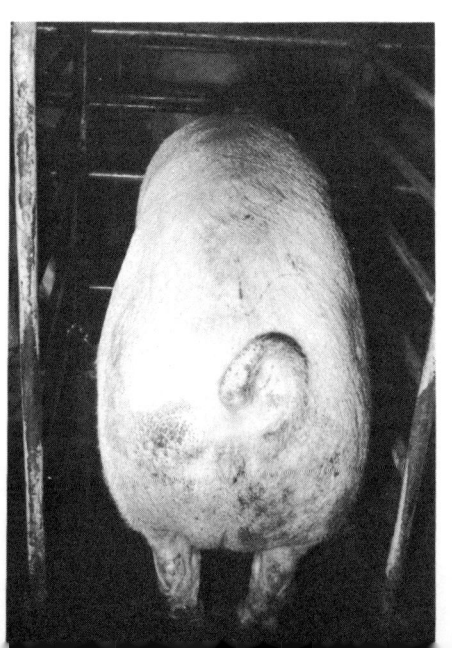

12. A little too fat.

SOW CONDITION

13. Milking off her back.

14. Much too thin—the 'thin sow syndrome'.

RESPONSES OF SOWS TO CHANGES IN NUTRIENT SUPPLY

The range of individual factors which characterise farms makes it difficult to specify in exact terms how a change in nutrition will effect performance. However, there is now a background of experimental data which allows the producer to predict how the productivity of the

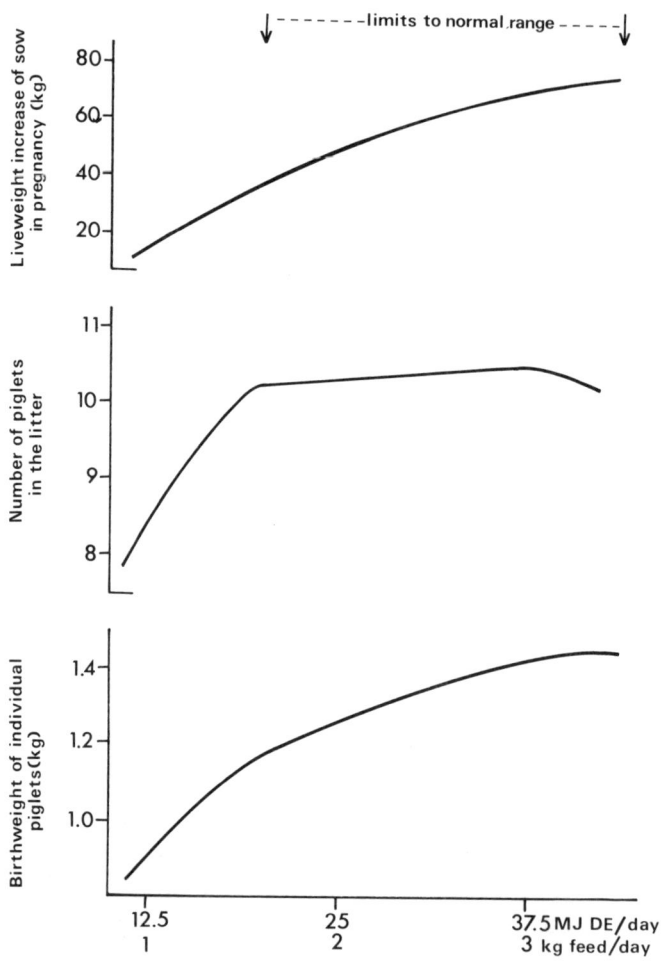

Figure 9.3. Effects of feed intake in pregnancy on sow productivity.

sows will react to changes in feed or protein intake.

These responses are shown in graphical form and represent no more than a best estimate of how the sow responds to changes in nutrition. There is no question of their being exactitudes, but with continuing research and development work, the accuracy with which these responses can be described will be progressively improved.

Feed intake in pregnancy (Figure 9.3)

The immediate and important effects of feed intake in pregnancy are upon birth weight, litter size and sow weight changes. It will be seen in Figure 9.3 that, above the level of 1.5 kg daily, there is a wide range of feed intake over which there is little effect in the number of pigs born, but there is a significant effect of feed intake on the birth weight of the pigs and this continues up to high levels of feeding. At very high levels of feeding, sows become over-fat and litter size may decrease. It also appears that the weight of the piglets becomes more variable, with a greater number of unusually heavy and of rather small pigs. The importance of birth weight lies in its effect on mortality during the first seven days of life rather than upon its effect on subsequent growth rate. Pigs less than 1 kg at birth are more likely to be born from sows with low feed intakes in pregnancy and these piglets are more liable to die. Mortality affects profitability so greatly that it is obviously worth-while considering if the birth weight can be increased by nutritional means. Figures 9.3 indicates that such an adjustment could be made, but only at considerable feed costs; a kilogram increase in the daily feed for every day of the pregnancy only leads to 0·2 kg increase in birth weight.

The changes in sow liveweight bear a simple relationship to changes in feed intake and represent both increases in the weight of the animal and increases in the percentage of fat in the sow.

Protein intake in pregnancy (Figure 9.4)

The graphs in Figure 9.4 indicate that over a wide range of intakes of digestible protein there is no influence of protein upon the number of pigs born or their birthweight. Differences in protein intake require to be extreme before differences in the composition of the pigs at birth or their viability are affected. On the other hand, sows are immature for the majority of their breeding life since they have not attained their target mature weight. It is therefore logical that additional protein intake will lead to some increase in the growth of the sow.

Feed intake in lactation (Figure 9.5)

Because body condition and the extent of the body fat stores are so crucial to lactation, the milk yield of sows is also affected by feed intake in pregnancy. Most important, however, is the feed intake in lactation. Figure 9.5 shows how both liveweight losses and milk yield

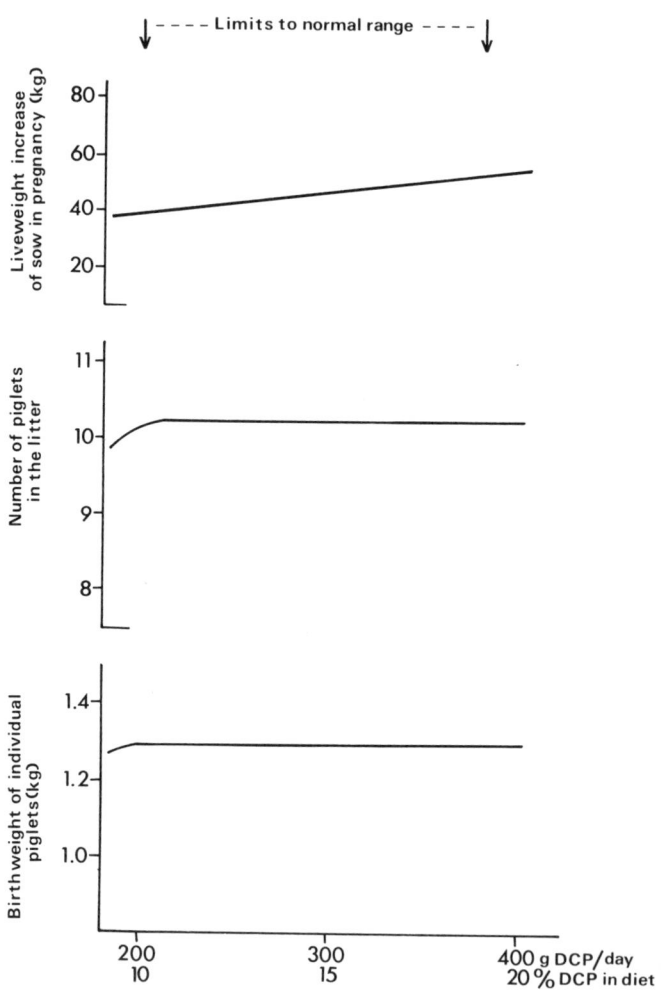

Figure 9.4. Effects of protein intake in pregnancy on sow productivity.

can be directly related to feed intake. This relationship becomes of greater importance as the sow becomes older and the body reserves of fat are used up. Figure 9.5 represents the situation in sows which have had two litters or more. For younger animals the relationship is less clear due to the sow having greater body reserves of fat.

Up to 21 days of age the growth of the piglets is related to the amount of the milk ingested by then. After 21 days of age, however,

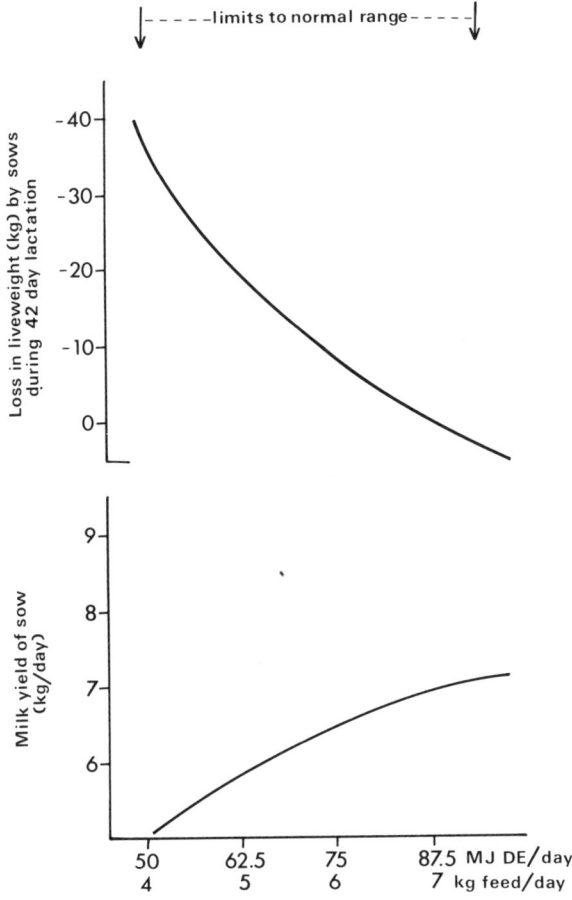

Figure 9.5. Effects of feed intake in lactation on milk yield and liveweight losses.

the amount of total feed ingested by the piglets becomes of greater importance, the total feed being a combination of mother's milk and of creep feed. The smaller the milk supply between three and six weeks, the greater the amount of creep that will be consumed by the litter in the same period. This balance between milk intake and creep feed may mean that the growth of the piglets receiving different quantities of milk, but with ready access to creep feed, may be similar. The importance of supplementary feed is closely associated with the age of weaning, since for piglets weaned at four weeks, milk intake is the dominant feature of their growth whilst with piglets weaned at eight weeks of age, creep consumption dictates how much greater than 13 kg the pig will weigh. Thirteen kilograms represent the average weight of pigs suckled up to eight weeks of age, but which were prevented from consuming any creep feed.

Protein intake in lactation

The evidence for a response in milk yield by the sow and in the growth of the pigs to changes in the intake of digestible crude protein by the sow is not conclusive. It is apparent that there is little to be gained from supplying in excess of 850 g DCP per day to lactating sows in respect of milk yield or piglet growth. Below 850 g, milk yield declines but the overall effect of this reduction is not apparent until an intake of 650 g DCP is reached, below which milk yield reduces rapidly. Logically, these comments should only be made after reference to the quality of the protein which is fed. However, there is insufficient knowledge to improve on the generalised, and inadequate, information already given in Table 3.3.

The sow has a limited capability to use body protein for purposes of synthesis of milk protein. Although this mechanism of providing milk protein is usually to be avoided, a reduction in the dietary intake of protein *will* increase the rate of liveweight loss by the sow. As is shown in Figure 9.6, these losses become of particular significance when diets containing less than 12 to 13 per cent DCP are given to lactating sows.

Sow liveweight and condition

Throughout, emphasis has been given to the importance and relevance of maternal body stores and growth in relation to sow productivity. The response of the sow in terms of body growth and composition to changes in feed intake is therefore crucial. The composition of these liveweight changes is of importance since the sow is divided between the wish to reach her target mature weight and the desirability of safeguarding the foetuses and milk production at the expense of her own body tissues. No accurate estimate of body

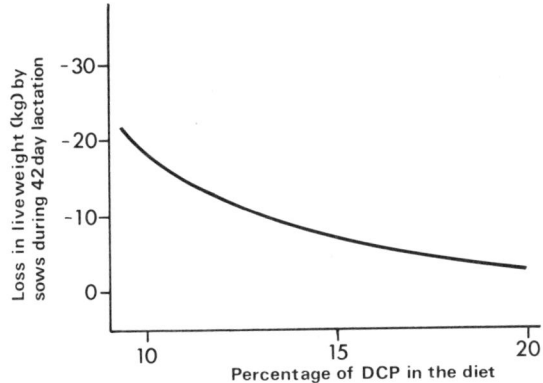

Figure 9.6. Effects of protein (DCP) intake in lactation on liveweight losses.

composition can be made under practical conditions, although a simple 'body score' is of some value.

The changes in body weight, particularly if they are related to the age of the sow, can be used to monitor nutritional adequacy, as has been previously described. They can also be used to evaluate the overall adequacy of the environment in which the sows are maintained, since a high disease incidence, for example, will be reflected in poor body gains relative to those of healthy sows.

In most cases body-weight changes are positively correlated with productivity, particularly the growth of the foetuses and milk production. The selection of optimum weight gains for sows remains the choice of the producer after taking into account effects of changes in sow performance upon the profitability of his unit. However, as an approximate guideline, sows which gain between 12 and 15 kg over each cycle from weaning to weaning are usually insured from the worst perils of nutritional inadequacy, but at the same time do not demand very high costs of production in terms of feed.

The most convenient point to weigh the sows is at mating, when the sow is individually moved and can be easily diverted onto a weighing machine. This weight can then be related to the weight obtained at a similar point in the previous cycle. More complete records of sow liveweight changes throughout pregnancy and lactation are rarely justified.

CHOOSING A PRE-MATING FEEDING PROGRAM

The level of feed intake selected between weaning and mating should allow the release of sufficient ova, their fertilisation and successful implantation. Within the limits shown in Figures 9.1 and 9.2 it is unlikely that feed intake prior to mating will greatly influence either ovulation or implantation.

Two situations have to be considered; firstly, the feed intake prior to mating of gilts, and secondly, the level of feed required by sows in the period from weaning and successful mating.

For the gilt, although it is apparent that the level of feeding can influence the number of eggs released and their subsequent fate, the normal ovulation rate in UK conditions, is sufficient for a litter of 12 piglets or so, and there is no necessity to increase the number of ova released by nutritional means. Rather the problem is embryo survival.

The situation can be complicated by a 'store period' following the selection of gilts at 80–90 kg for potential breeding stock. If gilts are fed below 22 MJ DE daily (1·8 kg per day), then an increase in feeding level for five days prior to mating will increase ovulation rate. If the gilts are fed about 30–32 MJ DE/day (2·5 kg per day) for a period of two weeks or so prior to mating, then still further increases in feed intake are unlikely to result in any increased ovulation rate or litter size.

In the case of sows, the length of the period from weaning to mating will depend on the length of the lactation period, since the average interval between weaning and oestrous falls from 8–10 days for sows weaned at 21 days to 3–5 days for sows weaned at 6–8 weeks. The greater the loss in liveweight during lactation the more important is the level of feeding between weaning and mating. Where the feed intake has allowed considerable liveweight losses in lactation, difficulty may be experienced in detecting signs of oestrous and of achieving fertilisation.

In normal circumstances about 2·5 kg of feed daily is appropriate between weaning and mating, but if the sow is in poor condition or has sustained heavy body weight losses in lactation, up to 4 kg can be given.

CHOOSING A FEEDING PROGRAM FOR BREEDING BOARS

The use of boars of 100 to 130 kg liveweight means that the boar has a considerable potential for growth during his effective breeding life, which is usually of up to four years' duration. Even if boars are fed considerably below their appetite levels, boars increase in liveweight—although the fat content of this gain is less than that of sows.

The ideal feeding regime would be one that maintains libido and semen production without also producing large body gains. This is rarely achieved, and in practice the diet provides for some liveweight gain. The energy burden of the production of the ejaculate is likely to be low, but strenuous sexual activity is more demanding in energy terms, as evidenced by the rapid loss of body weight and condition of boars used excessively. From practical experience it appears that boars are usually given about 250 to 350 g of digestible protein daily and 25 to 35 MJ DE daily. This may be provided by about 2·75 kg (6 lb) of an average lactating sow diet, but this intake will be far below the animal's appetite. The ration given to the boar should be adjusted according to his body condition, which should be kept lean.

PROCEDURE FOR CHOOSING THE FEEDING PROGRAM

Management

The first step should be to examine individual measures of sow productivity. As a basis of comparison these should be viewed against some target values, perhaps national or local standards of performance. Differences between the actual performance and the reference standard are often justifiable, but the presence of such differences should be recognised even although the simple existence of a difference is not necessarily a good reason for the producer to change his feeding program. However, many of the features of sow productivity which are resistant to nutritional factors are often more sensitive to management factors. Examples might be the conception rate, the number of pigs weaned, and the mortality of the newly born pigs, which are all more likely to be improved by alterations in management procedures than by changes in the nutritional program.

Deficiencies

Some obvious deficiencies of the nutritional program may be identified by clinical symptoms. For example, manifestations of vitamin A or pantothenic acid deficiencies may be sufficiently characteristic of the nutrient to allow specific remedial action to be taken. Where a nutritional deficiency is suspected, it may be worthwhile obtaining an analysis of the diet in respect of minerals, vitamins or amino acids. Gross misuse of mineral and vitamin supplements in the face of the manufacturer's advice is a likely source of an imbalanced or deficient diet. Less likely, is a lack of purity or availability of trace minerals or vitamins. Problems related to supposed amino acid deficiencies are more simply resolved by calculation of the amino acid composition of feed from accepted standard values applied to the ingredients. Only in unusual circumstances would one resort to the expensive and sophisticated approach of analysing the feed for its constituent amino acids.

Abuses

There are a range of broad performance characteristics which could be attributed to a nutritional abuse involving energy or protein. First, one should ascertain that actual feed intakes are within the limits specified in Figures 9.1 and 9.2. There may also be some disparity between the amount of food recorded as being offered and the amount the sow actually eats.

Having ascertained that the performance of the breeding herd is not subject to the more bizarre possibilities mentioned above, the choice of feeding program can be made on the basis of the sows' responses to changes in nutrient supply and with a view to achieving the levels of production required at minimum cost.

Indicators

The most obvious signs of a need to alter the pregnancy ration are a high post-natal mortality (above 10 per cent) or over-fat sows at farrowing. In lactation, piglet growth to three weeks of age is a reflection of milk production by the sow. From three to six weeks, piglet growth relates to the intake of milk and creep feed combined. The rate of sow weight losses in lactation indicates the adequacy of lactation feeding, while failure to re-breed successfully within five days of weaning can be indicative of a more general failure to meet the sow's nutritional needs.

Within the broad limits of nutrient supply to the sow which would avoid gross symptoms such as these, it remains to select the optimum feeding regime. The most effective way of monitoring the effects of the feeding program upon the sow herd is by examining the liveweight changes of the sows. Not only does the change in liveweight from weaning to weaning give a good picture of the adequacy of feeding under the particular conditions of individual units, but liveweight change is also closely related to sow productivity.

Action

By examination of weight changes from weaning to weaning, two values may be derived: (1) The average weight change for the sows, and (2) The variation between individual sows in the amount of weight gained. The average weight change found may be compared to the target value appropriate for individual circumstances (a minimum of 12–15 kg has been suggested). This will indicate the adequacy of the overall feeding program, and whether any adjustment is required.

The extent of the variation in weight changes between sows reflects the range of environments to which individual sows have been subjected. The more variable the weight-change responses of sows to apparently similar feed intakes, the more necessary it is to control the feeding program of sows individually.

Liveweight changes of sows are most readily influenced when the sows can be individually fed; that is, in pregnancy and also between weaning and mating. A guide to the amounts of food needed to bring about various different rates of gain in pregnancy have been given in Table 7.2.

After a sow has given four or five litters, it is necessary to stabilise her body weight at 180 kg or so (when weighed at weaning). Otherwise, the sow will go on growing towards her target mature weight of 250 to 300 kg. For sows attaining these higher liveweights, special allowances must be made for their increased maintenance costs.

If any change is made in the herd management in respect to environment, buildings, disease control or type of pig, it is probable that the feeding program will also need to be altered. A striking example of the need for this is to be found in Figure 9.7 which shows the effects of level of feed intake in pregnancy upon the birth weight of piglets. It is apparent that the individual effects of each farm bring

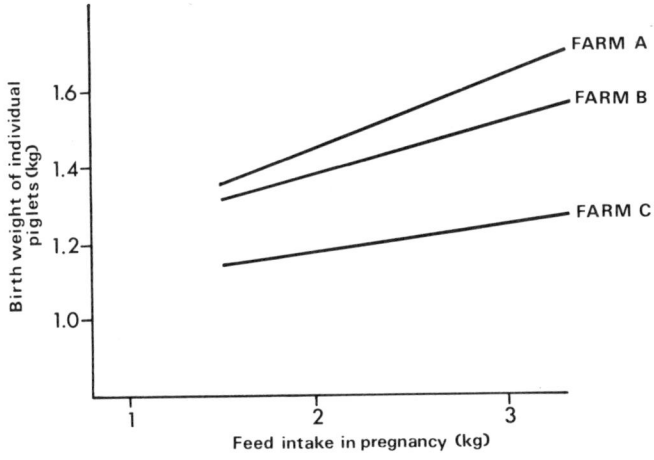

Figure 9.7. Effects of feed intake in pregnancy upon the birthweight of piglets on three separate farms.

about marked differences in response. Thus, under the conditions pertaining at Farm C, an individual birth weight of 1·2 kg could be achieved at a pregnancy intake of 2·5 kg daily, while the same weight at birth on Farm A could be achieved on an intake of less than 2 kg. Similarly, if the sows are kept under conditions where the season of the year is of importance, then the feeding program in winter must allow for the extra food needed to satisfy the increased nutritive load of the environment.

Chapter 10

FEEDSTUFFS

QUANTITATIVE KNOWLEDGE of the nutritive value of feed ingredients is essential, because feedstuffs are incorporated into pig diets in substitution for, and in complement with, other feedstuffs. The relative values of different feeds can then be compared and the nutrients contained in them purchased at the lowest cost. Feeds can then be combined together to provide the pig's requirements for protein, energy and the other nutrients, and the response of the pig to the feedstuff can be predicted.

We need to know of a feedstuff: Does it contain toxins? Is it palatable? Can the pig eat enough of it within the physical limits of gut fill to satisfy energy needs? How much energy is there? How much energy is digested? How much protein is there? How much protein is digested? How useful is the digested protein for synthesis of new protein within the pig? How much of the digested energy is in the protein? What is the mineral and vitamin compostion? Does it contain any peculiar positive or negative characteristics? How well does it store?

To characterise feeds and answer the questions posed above, two types of study are needed. Chemical tests are carried out on the feed to determine its constituent parts, then the feed is given to pigs to examine how the pig itself responds to it.

THE METABOLISM STUDY

Figure 10.1 shows a pig eating 1 kg of feed. The most difficult aspect of metabolism to measure is the heat loss from the body; to measure heat losses, a complicated and expensive energy balance chamber which measures heat output is needed. However, for the purposes of feed evaluation in terms of the practical nutrition of the pig, knowledge of heat losses are not essential. Feed evaluation procedures do not usually need to take account either of losses of nitrogen or energy from the pig in gases escaping from the mouth or anus. All that is left to measure is the input of energy and protein in the feed and the output of energy and protein in the urine and faeces.

Metabolism trials

Figure 10.2 opposite shows the metabolism crate into which the pig has to be placed for a feed evaluation study. The various features of the crate are designed to ensure that the quantity of food eaten is exactly known, that the urine and faeces are all completely collected and that neither of these three fractions contaminate any of the others.

The male pig is usually used owing to the convenient physical separation in that sex of anus and penis. He is restrained front and rear to prevent the forward/backward movement which would allow the pig to urinate into the faeces container or defaecate into the urine box. Feed is given in the trough which is specially deep, and there is

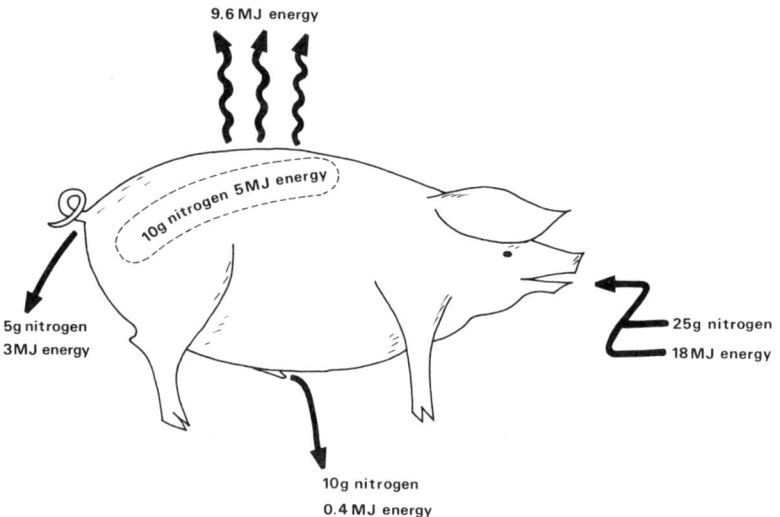

Figure 10.1. Measurements for a metabolism study.

Energy in feed (18 MJ GE) less energy in faeces (3 MJ) gives the digestible energy (15 MJ DE/kg diet). The digestibility coefficient for energy is 15/18 = 0·83 or 83 per cent. DE less energy in urine (0·4 MJ) gives the metabolisable energy (14·6 MJ ME/kg diet). ME is 97 per cent of DE and 81 per cent of GE. ME less energy lost as heat (9·6 MJ) gives 5MJ of energy retained in the tissues of the body.

Nitrogen in feed (25 g N) less nitrogen in faeces (5 g N) gives 20 g of digestible nitrogen (DN) in the diet. The digestibility coefficient for nitrogen (and protein) is 20/25 = 0·80 or 80 per cent. Digestible nitrogen x 6·25 = digestible crude protein (DCP) which is 125 g DCP/kg diet or 12·5 per cent DCP. Nitrogen digested (20 g) less nitrogen in urine (10 g) gives 10 g nitrogen retained or 62·5 g protein retained, or about 275 g of lean growth.

Of the 5 MJ energy retained, 1·5 MJ is in the protein and 3·5 MJ in fat, giving about 100 g of fat growth.

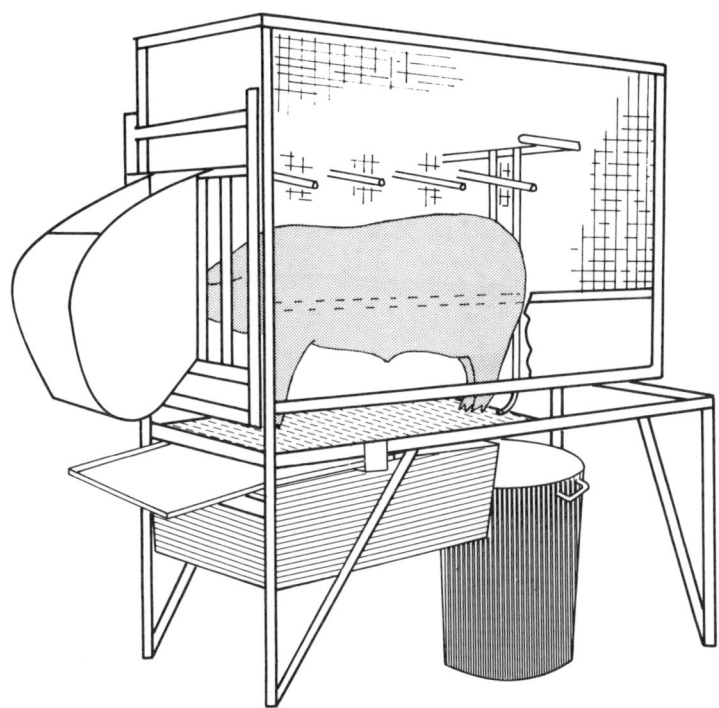

Figure 10.2. Metabolism crate for growing pigs.

a tray underneath to catch spilt food and prevent it falling into the urine box. The urine falls directly through the open mesh of the cage floor into the urine box and the faeces fall over the back of the mesh into the bin.

Usually, the routine is to feed and collect for two periods, each of about 10 days, building up the faeces and urine in their containers and using sulphuric acid to stop any growth of mould or losses of nitrogen in the form of ammonia. The total collections of urine and of faeces are thoroughly stirred before sampling, Then, the samples of faeces, urine and feed are analysed individually.

In Table 10.1 are shown two sets of results from metabolism trials in which maize and barley or fish meal and fish silage were examined. Energy-rich cereals are fed together with a protein-rich basal diet and cereals are used as the basal diet for protein-rich feeds. The energy in the diet containing 50 per cent maize is more digestible than energy in the diet containing 50 per cent barley. In the case of the fish

TABLE 10.1. Some results from a metabolism study showing the digestibility of mixed diets and single feedstuffs

	Diet containing 50% of a protein-rich supplement together with:		Diet containing 75% of an energy-rich supplement together with:	
	50% maize	50% barley	25% fish meal	25% fish silage
Digestibility of energy (%)	85	82	81	83
Digestibility of nitrogen (%)	86	85	89	91
Efficiency of nitrogen retention (%)	42	40	33	38

	Maize	Barley	Fish meal	Fish silage
Digestible energy value (MJ DE/kg DM)[1]	16·1	14·7	15·7	17·9
Digestible nitrogen value (g DN/kg DM)	16·0	13·1	112	119

[1] Feed values may be given either on the basis of concentration in the dry matter (DM) or of concentration in the foodstuff as fed to the pig

comparison, the efficiency of retention is lower for the diet containing 25 per cent fish meal; it appears that the protein is a little less digestible, and also less well utilised.

The nutritional value of the feedstuff itself, rather than the diet, may be determined by a difference calculation. First, the digestibility of the basal diet is determined. Next, the feedstuff under examination is added into the basal diet, preferably at a series of inclusion rates (for example, 10, 20 and 30 per cent for protein feeds; 25, 50 and 75 per cent for energy feeds). The digestibility value for the mixed diet is used, together with that for basal diet, to calculate the digestibility of the test ingredient. To find the digestible energy (DE) value and the digestible nitrogen (DN) value, the calculated digestibility coefficient is multiplied by the analysed concentration of energy and nitrogen in the feedstuff. These values are given in the bottom half of Table 10.1. If the value for digestible crude protein (DCP) rather than DN is required, the DN concentration is multiplied by 6·25.

CHEMICAL METHODS

Clearly, the major determinant of the amount of digestible energy and digestible nitrogen in a feed is the quantity of energy and nitrogen that the feed contains. Next is the quantity of fibre in the feed, fibre being a major influence upon digestibility. Protein losses as nitrogen in the urine are greatly affected by the quality of feed protein; that is, the content, balance and digestibility of amino acids. If chemical determination for essential amino acids, particularly for available lysine, is added to the other chemically determined values, then a reasonable estimate of the value of a feed may be made. The estimate may be particularly close if a feed has been fully evaluated by use of metabolism studies at some earlier date. In that case, the chemical analysis is used to ascertain that there is no reason to suspect a current feed batch will behave in the pig any differently from previous batches. The normal form is to examine a new food by use of both metabolism and chemical analysis, and then subsequently to check out the feed at regular intervals only with chemical analysis.

Recently, the protein quality has been expressed in shorthand form with a statement of the concentration of lysine. Lysine is only one of the 10 or so essential amino acids, and protein quality is better stated if the concentration of methionine + cystine is also known. It is now currently in vogue to include threonine, but ideally a statement is needed about the concentration of all the essential amino acids. This more nearly resembles the concept of biological value, which expresses fully the quality of the protein in a feedstuff. Biological value may be determined by looking at the efficiency with which digested protein is retained in the body. Unfortunately, as has been described in Figure 3.1–6, knowledge of the biological values of individual feed ingredients does not necessarily supply an accurate indication of the biological value of the protein in a diet containing a mixture of feedstuffs. In order to measure diet quality in relation to this important factor affecting animal response to protein intake, it would be necessary to test every diet by use of a live pig metabolism study. The vast number of diets being used currently by the UK pig industry makes this quite impracticable.

The need, therefore, is for a value which can be attached to a mixed diet, but which is calculated from the amino acid composition of the various separate feed ingredients of that diet. To determine all the amino acids in feed ingredients is arduous but relatively simple, and to calculate the amino acids in a diet made up of a number of ingredients is also a simple process. Biological value can now be estimated from the final amino acid balance determined for each individual mixed diet.

TABLES OF FEED VALUES

Tables which may be used as a guide to the nutritive values of feedstuffs for pigs are given in Appendices 2 and 3. The information in Appendix 2 is arranged to be appropriate for the formulation of pig diets and to predict pig responses. Appendix 3 can be used for determining the amino acid composition (biological value) of a mixed diet made up of the various ingredients.

The tables do not purport to be either comprehensive or exact. Where the precise value of a food is needed, the definitive answer cannot be assumed to be found in these tables. Some feedstuffs are so difficult to define and so variable in quality that a printed value in a table can be very misleading. For a new feedstuff, a metabolism study is essential to determine at least digestibility of energy and nitrogen. Chemical determinations are more simple and are undertaken routinely by mills producing compound feeds for sale, and by larger pig producers. A comprehensive service for the chemical analysis of feeds is also provided by advisory services. The nutritive values given in Appendices 2 and 3 are no substitute for metabolism studies and chemical analysis of samples from the feedstuff itself—particularly when the latter service is so readily available on request to local advisory bodies. In the absence of either of these, however, the tables may be useful as a guide.

Many feedstuffs vary between batches and frequent analysis can pay dividends. Barley, the basis of UK pig diets, usually contains between 8 and 12 per cent crude protein. A diet based on the 8 per cent barley may need 20 per cent of soya-bean meal adding to it; a diet based on the 12 per cent barley would only need about 10 per cent of soya for the mixed diet to be of equal protein content. A wrong assumption in these cases could be expensive either in wasted soya or in failure to attain optimum lean growth.

To ensure that the chemical analysis for a batch of a feedstuff is correct, the sampling procedure must be thorough. A sample sent to the laboratory for analysis may only weigh 5 kg or so, but the bulk from which it was taken could be many tonnes. If the sample is not representative of the whole bulk, the analysis can be more misleading than a value in a set of tables such as Appendix 2.

The nutritive values of proprietary pre-mixes are not given in Appendix 2 as these are best obtained from the compounder of the pre-mix direct. Protein pre-mixes containing 40–60 per cent of crude protein are available for the supplementation of cereals, and fat pre-mixes with about 50 per cent fat are useful for increasing the energy concentration of diets.

Tables of nutritive values can be improved by regular up-dating. Much of the variations in cereal analysis is caused by nitrogen fertilisation, season (year) and district of origin. Nutritive values of feedstuffs given on a regional and annual basis are available from advisory services and are invaluable to pig production units which grow or buy-in local grain for home mixing.

FEEDING TRIALS

The last step in the feed evaluation procedure is to give the feedstuff to pigs under normal conditions and to carefully monitor the response. This is the final element of nutrient evaluation—not the first. The feeding trial ascertains that actual responses are as they would be predicted from chemical analysis and metabolism study. Although the feeding trial cannot, by itself, effectively evaluate a feedstuff, the user of any set of feed analyses is unlikely to have faith in them until the values given have been validated by feeding trials. For conventional feedstuffs, years of commercial use serve as a validation, but for new or unconventional feedstuffs specific experiments are required to verify results from chemical tests and metabolism studies.

Inclusion of a feedstuff at low levels is unlikely to give interpretable results in a feeding trial. Thus, if 5 per cent of a diet as one feed is substituted for 5 per cent of the diet as another feed and there is no difference in growth response, this does *not* mean the two feeds are of equal value. It is as likely that the experiment simply was not sensitive enough to show up the difference. The unwary may arrive at the conclusion that sand has equal nutritional value to maize! Care must also be taken with the response parameter chosen. For example, reproductive performance in the pregnant sow is very unresponsive to dietary protein and protein sources are best compared by using young growing pigs.

The feeding and growth trial does, however, have the advantage that the feedstuff under test can be examined for long periods of time under normal conditions. Not until this has been done can one be sure that the chemical analyses and metabolism studies have apportioned the correct value to the feed.

UNUSUAL FEEDSTUFFS

Until recently, ingredients for pig diets in the United Kingdom have been derived from a very conservative range of about half a dozen well-tried ingredients. The changing economic climate and world food supply situation is forcing the industry into a more catholic view of potential feedstuffs for pig diets. Many unusual feedstuffs are unusual simply because they have not yet been comprehensively tested. Given that the tests are properly completed, there is reason to hope that a wider range of ingredients will be commonly included into pig diets. There is particular scope for the new protein sources from micro-organisms (bacteria and yeasts) and fungi, high density feedstuffs for growing pigs and low density feedstuffs for finishing pigs and pregnant sows.

There is also a wide range of feedstuffs that have been traditionally used for pig diets but for which accurate descriptions are not available. This is because the feeds have not been available in large quantities, or were of such variability that comprehensive evaluation was not justified. For example, by-products of the bakery trade, milk by-products, chicken offal and a range of root crops such as beet and carrots. Many of these potential feedstuffs can have physical or contamination problems and simple chemical analysis may well fail to adequately categorise them.

Grazing

Grass, clover, lucerne and other crops may be effectively grazed and satisfactorily utilised by pigs; particularly by sows. The problem is complicated by a relationship with stage of maturity; the digestibility of the energy in grass can change from 70 per cent for young grass at the 6 leaf stage to a value of 30 per cent for mature grass. Feed intake is difficult to determine and is related to the availability of other foodstuffs such as concentrates. The actual intake of the grazing sow is difficult to quantify, but it is unlikely to exceed 6 MJ DE per day.

Fibrous feedstuffs
The nutritive values of all feeds of low nutrient density are imperfectly known. Such feeds present problems in that they are more than usually variable in nutritive composition. Any estimate of the net nutritive contribution is further complicated by the fibrous nature of such feeds interfering with the digestion of other diet components. Whilst the adult pig has the undoubted ability to digest roughages in the caecum and large intestine, the extent to which the pig breaks down, absorbs and utilises fibrous feeds has yet to be quantified accurately.

In view of the potential of low density feedstuffs for pigs, these shortcomings in our knowledge must be remedied in the near future.

Chapter 11

DIET FORMULATION

FEED COMPOUNDING, or more precisely, diet formulation, matches the needs of the pig with the nutrients in its daily feed supply. There are five elements to consider: the nutrient requirements of the pig, the nutritive value of the feed ingredients, the nutrient concentration required in the mixed diet, the feedstuffs chosen to make up the finally formulated diet, and the amount of the diet that the pig is given as its daily ration.*

Nutrient requirement can be stated in terms of digested energy, digested protein, quality of protein digested, essential amino acids, minerals and vitamins. An example of a set of nutrient requirements which might be appropriate for a growing pig is given in Table 11.1.

The concentration of nutrients in the various feedstuffs are stated in the same terms as those which defined the animal's nutrient requirement. These are in Appendix 2.

The specification for the nutritive content of the diet is in Table 11.2.

The diet formulation concerns the quantities of the various feedstuffs which are to be mixed together into the final diet in such proportion to each other that the nutrient concentrations given in Table 11.2 are all achieved. An example of a diet formulation is shown in Table 11.3.

Finally, the amount of the diet that the pig is to receive daily must be stated in order that the daily requirement shown in Table 11.1 is matched with the mixed diet of Table 11.3. In the case given, the

---

*There is often some confusion about the terms *ration*, *diet* and *requirement*. The pig has a nutrient requirement for energy, protein, minerals and vitamins, the requirement is expressed on a daily basis. For example, a growing pig might require 26 MJ of DE daily.

The *diet formulation* states the proportion in which feedstuffs must be added together to make up a mixed *diet*. For example, 75 per cent barley, 25 per cent soya-bean meal.

The *nutrient specification* for the diet describes the concentration of the various nutrients in the diet. For example, 13 MJ DE/kg.

The *ration* is the amount of diet fed to the pig daily. By controlling the intake of the diet, the ration ensures that the daily supply of nutrients from the diet satisfies the nutrient requirement. For example, 2 kg of a diet containing 13 MJ DE/kg will supply 26 MJ DE daily.

If rationed, the diet is *fed* a number of times daily. Sometimes *feed* is used as a familiar term for diet and occasionally as a shortened form of the word feedstuff.

DIET FORMULATION

TABLE 11.1 Nutrient requirements for a growing pig (required per day)

Digestible energy (DE)	26 MJ
Digestible crude protein (DCP)	280 g [1]
Lysine	14 g
Methionine + cystine	10 g
Calcium	16 g
Phosphorus	12 g

[1] DCP of biological value 65 or above

TABLE 11.2. Specification for the nutrient content of a growing pig diet (per kg of mixed diet)

Digestible energy (DE)	13 MJ	
Digestible crude protein (DCP)	140 g	(14·0%)
Lysine	7 g	(0·7%)
Methionine + cystine	5 g	(0·5%)
Calcium	8 g	(0·8%)
Phosphorus	6 g	(0·6%)
Vitamin and trace elements	3 g	(0·3%)

TABLE 11.3. Formulation of ingredients for a growing pig diet (kg/tonne of mixed diet)

Fish meal	20	(2%)
Extracted soya bean	75	(7·5%)
Wheat offals	290	(29%)
Barley	200	(20%)
Wheat	300	(30%)
Maize meal	70	(7%)
Decorticated cotton seed	25	(2·5%)
Calcium carbonate	12	(1·2%)
Di-calcium phosphate	4	(0·4%)
Vitamin and trace element supplement	3	(0·3%)

ration allowance is 2 kg of diet daily. If the animal is to be fed twice daily the feed allowance is 1 kg.

Additivity

When compounding diets for pigs it is assumed that the nutrients from the various feedstuffs act in an additive manner. That is, the nutritive value of a mixed diet is the sum of the nutritive values of the various ingredients.

If a pig eats 6 MJ of barley DE and 5 MJ of maize DE, he is assumed to have digested 11 MJ of DE. This assumption is generally justified, and greatly simplifies diet formulation.

Occasionally, there may be cause to doubt the general rule. Particularly if: (1) the DE value attributed to the feedstuff is suspected to vary according to the amount eaten, (2) the feed ingredient is of low nutrient density, or (3) a single feedstuff is included at high level.

The most controversial case currently, is that of the high fibre feedstuffs: oats, wheat offals and grass meals. At high levels of inclusion, do these feeds have the same DE values as at lower levels of inclusion? Possibly not, if a part of the DE is derived from microbial fermentation. Further, do high fibre feeds interact in the diet and reduce the digestibility of the other feed ingredients? Possibly so, if they prevent enzymes permeating fully into the food mass or increase the metabolic faecal losses.

The same assumptions of additivity are made for protein; 150 g DCP from soya bean and 50 g DCP from fish meal is assumed to equal 200 g DCP. As for energy, this convenient generalisation is usually correct. However, there are the same doubts as with energy concerning the lower density feedstuffs and unconventional feeds. In addition, there have been some notorious cases of non-additivity when feeds containing protease inhibitor activity were used in diets; raw potato, for example. In this instance the protease inhibitor influences the digestible protein content of the whole diet, not just the potato.

In diet formulation DCP is of limited usefulness without a direct measure of the biological value of the protein mixture, or at least an indicator of biological value from the levels of some amino acids. Biological value is not additive, so adding together the biological value of diet ingredients will not give the biological value of the mixed diet. This must be determined separately for each diet.

Units of measurement for diet formulation

The use of digestible energy (DE) values for feed formulation assumes that the main differences between sources of energy in the various feedstuffs is related to digestibility. The gross energy in wheat offal, for example, is similar to the gross energy in maize, but because wheat offal is only 70 per cent digestible, whereas maize is 90 per cent digestible, there are large and important differences in the amount of energy which the pig effectively obtains from these two ingredients. The use of DE to classify feeds rather than metabolisable energy (ME) prevents any preconceptions about energy losses in urine. These are variable, and are a function of the animal, protein quality and rate of total protein supply.

Very frequently, pig diets are formulated on the basis of crude protein (CP) rather than digestible crude protein (DCP) or digestible N (DN). To do *this* is to predispose the system to an unnecessary degree of error, as it fails to allow for differences in digestibility of

FEEDING

15. Grazing can provide 6MJ DE, or none.

16. A mill and mix unit with a throughput of about 2 tonne/hour.

protein. To allow for those differences for energy, but then to not allow for the same differences for protein, is irrational behaviour. The CP, rather than DCP convention, arose as a result of most of our traditional protein sources possessing similar digestibility values for their protein.

Lysine is the most frequently used indicator of biological value as it is invariably the first-limiting amino acid in cereal-based pig diets. This, whilst convenient, is not without dangers. To use the lysine content of a diet as the statement of protein quality is to imply that lysine will solve any amino acid balance problems that the dietary protein might possess. Ultimately, the pig requires all the essential amino acids in a particular balance and at a particular total level. This need may only be quantified by a statement of total DCP supply together with a measure of the biological value for that DCP.

In order to reduce the dangers of using lysine as the sole measure of protein quality, methionine plus cystine is often also considered since the sulphur amino acids are often second-limiting in cereal-based pig diets. In maize-based diets tryptophan may be the second-limiting amino acid. Currently, there is a suggestion that threonine might be the second- or third-limiting amino acid in pig diets, and in this case threonine should be included. Logically, as the deficiency of each individual amino acid is recognised, each becomes in sequence the next limiting. When the last essential amino acid is included one will have, *de facto*, a statement of biological value.

For purposes of diet formulation the mineral elements are usually stated in terms of their level of total elements, rather than the level of available element. This practice is particularly likely to lead to error where a high proportion of the needs of the animal appear to to be met from sources which turn out to be less well absorbed than was originally assumed. This situation would apply for some rock phosphates, and plant phosphates, for example. The stated requirements of the pig for phosphorus usually assumes an overall diet availability of phosphorus of about 50 per cent, and at least some monitoring of the type of phosphorus in the diet ingredients is needed to ensure that there is no deficiency such as might result from diet phosphorus being unavailable to the animal.

The daily ration forms the link between the diet specification as provided by the ingredient formulation, and the nutrient requirement of the animal in terms of its daily needs. Thus, the product of diet concentration and ration (diet × ration) gives the daily nutrient supply. (For example, 13 MJ DE/kg × 2 kg/day gives 26 MJ DE. 140 g DCP/kg (14% DCP) × 2 kg/day gives 280 g DCP).

The statement of nutrient requirement assumes that this can be strictly defined. Such an attempt has been made in the foregoing chapters; but these chapters will also have served to suggest that, as yet, the practical nutrition of the pig is an imperfect science. Nutrient need is a function of the productivity that is required from the animal. The first act of the feed compounder must be to define the productivity required and then to determine those nutrient needs which will provide for the target production level. Only then can a diet be formulated to fulfil the specific production objective for which it was designed.

Since a diet must be prepared with a view to the requirements of the pig, and since the requirements of the pig are a function of the production objectives of the pig producer, there are likely to be a great number of different diets needed.

It is quite impossible for there to be any generally-applicable requirement for nutrients by pigs. Equally it is impossible for any single diet to be universally suitable for all pigs of any particular type; all growing pigs, for example, or all pregnant sows.

The optimum diet formulations for any pig production unit is likely to be an individual characteristic of that unit and not necessarily applicable to other units.

HAND CALCULATION

In Table 11.4 is a worksheet set up for formulating a diet which is to have a final concentration of 13 MJ DE/kg, 12 per cent DCP and 0·70 per cent total lysine. The calculation of biological value is arduous by hand; so, for purposes of example, the amino acid lysine will be used as an indicator of protein quality. The worksheet has been given letters against each row and numbers against each column. The specification for the desired diet is to be found along row Z. The work has been simplified by choosing only three nutrients; DE, DCP and lysine. A further simplification has been the selection of only three feedstuffs—barley, wheat and fish meal (column 2). The DE, DCP and lysine concentration of the three ingredients on the worksheet are given in columns 3, 5 and 7.

A start is made at row A by selecting a likely combination; say 75 per cent barley, 10 per cent wheat and 12 per cent fish meal (column 1). This totals to 97 per cent, leaving 3 per cent for minerals and a trace element and vitamin mix. The contribution of energy to the diet (column 4) made by barley is 75 per cent of 12·7, $12·7 \times 0·75 = 9·5$. The contribution of wheat is $14 \times 0·10 = 1·4$, and that of fish meal 1·8. These sum to $9·5 + 1·4 + 1·8 = 12·7$ MJ DE. The contribution of DCP to the diet (column 6) made by barley is $7·7 \times 0·75 = 5·8$, the contribution from wheat and fish meal are 0·8 and 7·0 respectively, making a total of 13·6 per cent DCP. The total dietary lysine (column 8) similarly calculated is 0·8 per cent. In relation to

TABLE 11.4. Worksheet for hand calculation of a diet

	1	2	3	4	5	6	7	8
			DE (MJ/kg)		DCP (%)		Lysine (%)	
	% inclusion	ingredient	in ingredient	in diet	in ingredient	in diet	in ingredient	in diet
A	75	Barley	12·7	9·5	7·7	5·8	0·32	0·24
	10	Wheat	14·0	1·4	8·3	0·8	0·28	0·03
	12	Fish meal	15·1	1·8	58	7·0	4·60	0·55
				12·7		13·6		0·82
B	62	Barley		7·9		4·8		0·20
	26	Wheat		3·6		2·2		0·07
	9	Fish meal		1·4		5·2		0·41
				12·9		12·2		0·68
Z	100	Final diet		13		12		0·70

the target values (row Z), the first attempt (row A) is low in energy, high in protein and high in lysine. The next attempt made is shown at row B. This tests a reduced inclusion of fish meal and increased inclusion of wheat. With 62 per cent barley, 26 per cent wheat and 9 per cent fish meal the specification for the final diet is now closely approached. To get three nutrients correctly balanced in a three-ingredient diet usually takes about four or five attempts. If the dietary specification includes five or six nutrients, and if there are 15 or so available feedstuffs, the number of attempts that have to be made before one achieves the right balance of nutrients in the final diet escalates dramatically.

Some on-farm feed formulation problems

The reaction of a formulator to a dietary ingredient list depends upon his circumstances. Where automatic weighing machines are available, where the movement of materials is mechanised and where large quantities of diets are to be mixed, it is a simple matter to add together large numbers of ingredients each at a low level. Similarly, unusual and unrounded quantities (260 kg (580 lb), for example) can be readily incorporated. For many on-farm mixing facilities, such opportunities cannot be exploited. The purchase of many small lots of minor ingredients can lead to increased costs, both for the raw materials themselves, and in storage and handling costs. The strongest objection to multi-ingredient diet formulations is simply the confusion that is caused in a small facility.

The number of ingredients available on the farm may be limited to home-grown barley together with a single purchased protein source (eg, soya-bean meal). As even the most simple mix requires some minor ingredients; for example di-calcium phosphate, and a ready-mixed vitamin and trace element supplement, there is a minimum of four ingredients to a single diet. This number may be reduced down to two or three by the purchase of a proprietary protein concentrate which also includes minerals, vitamins and possibly some other additives, and has a protein level and amino acid balance compounded to be suitable for cereal supplementation.

In the preparation of these proprietary protein concentrate mixes, the commercial firm has not invoked supernatural powers, not effected any mix which the enterprising pig producer could not do for himself. The commercial firm may, however, purchase ingredients more cheaply by buying in bulk, and can also offer to the home-mixer a convenient, trouble-free service.

Some farm-mixing facilities allow only one hundredweight (50 kg) units, so all ingredients are most conveniently included if they are used at a minimum of 50 kg and in units of 50 kg. If the arrangements are such that the cereals can be weighed in 50 kg units from a bulk store, but the supplementary ingredients are tipped direct into the mixer, then the bag size governs the unit size for the inclusion rate. Soya-bean meal, for example, often comes in 140 lb (64 kg) bags.

Unfortunately sacrifices are often made in the name of convenience which results in incorrect diet formulation and a failure to exploit cheap ingredients when they are available.

Ingredient restraints

Consideration of the fitness of an ingredient for a diet extends beyond its nutrient content. Some of these aspects are noted in Appendix 2.

For the pig's part, the ingredient must be palatable, not contain any toxic factors, and not over-fill the intestine.

For the producer's part the ingredient must not taint the flesh, produce soft fat, fill the slurry chambers, or be particularly dusty.

For the compounder's part, the ingredient must be readily available in the required quantities, and must not be unpredictable in composition, so bulky as to raise transport problems, of poor storage characteristics, other than freeflowing, difficult to form into pellets, form into pellets which are too hard, or produce adverse reactions when handled.

In many cases feed ingredients with doubtful pedigrees are restricted in their rates of inclusion. Sometimes these restraints have arisen as a result of feeding experiments which have shown no deleterious effects below a certain level, but some evidence of reduced performance above that level. It is possible that for some feeds there really is a certain inclusion rate below which the ingredient is impeccable but above which it becomes less useful. It is also probable that the deleterious effects of a dietary ingredient become less as the inclusion rate falls, and below a certain level of inclusion the experimental procedures are simply unable to measure those effects.

Unpredictability in the nutritive quality of an ingredient may also be masked if the inclusion rate is low. If, for example, a batch of meat and bone meal has been heat damaged, an inclusion rate of 2–3 per cent will not be a disaster. If all the supplementary protein in the diet was as meat and bone, however, the effect upon pig growth would be severe. There is safety in a large number of ingredients included at low rates.

Other reasons for limiting the inclusion rate of an ingredient in a diet will include particular problems relating to feed texture. High levels of fine-ground wheat, for example, may cause an indigestible paste to form in the pig's stomach. Finely-ground cereals in general may predispose the pig to gastric ulcers. The influences of high fibre feeds, such as wheat offals, often precludes inclusions above 25 per cent. This is not just because of effects on metabolic faecal nitrogen, which are accounted for in the DCP value, but also because the responses of pigs to diets which include high levels of feed ingredients such as these are not yet well enough known.

It is also the case that some ingredients are always included into diets at a stated minimum level. For example, some compounders may feel that fish meal attributes special qualities to the diet; in these circumstances a minimum inclusion rate of 2·5 per cent might be insisted upon—regardless of price. Similarly, barley may be included in all diets, again regardless of price, at a level of about 25–30 per cent, in order to maintain continuity between formulations. The circumstance that a minimum inclusion rate is designed to alleviate, is where, because of a change in price structure, a fattening unit previously using a diet of maize and fish meal suddenly receives a new diet of wheat and soya.

Although some ingredient restraints for feedstuffs are given in Appendix 2, these are not recommended restraints. Where diet ingredients are cheap, the more courageous feed compounder may be well rewarded. What constitutes an ingredient restraint is often as much opinion as biological reasoning.

COMPUTER CALCULATION—LEAST COST DIET FORMULATION

The computer gives rapid solution of arithmetical problems. This facility improves the efficiency of diet formulation. Although the same rules apply as for the hand calculation, when the computer does the maths there is no limit to the number of ingredients which can be examined for dietary inclusion. Neither is there any limit to the nutritional characteristics which may be taken into account, so it is possible to juggle with ingredients to get out exactly the right nutrient concentrations that have been specified for any particular diet. This is not to say that the computer selects all the ingredients, normally at least two-thirds of available ingredients price themselves out of the mix, and are not used.

The computer can also run a linear program for least-cost. This routine demands not only that the available ingredients are mixed to provide the exact diet specification requested, but this is done for the minimum cost. Clearly, a particular balance of energy, protein, amino acids and minerals could be reached by a number of different ingredient combinations. But only one particular ingredient recipe will achieve the nutrient specification at the least possible cost. The least-cost recipe will change frequently, as the relative prices of feedstuffs change. When maize is cheap per unit DE, then least-costed diets will be high in maize. If the price of maize energy rises relative to the price of barley energy, the diets will no longer contain maize, but barley instead.

The greater the freedom of choice given to the computer, the better the chance of reducing the price of the diet. The efficiency of the program will be improved if only a lower limit is set for a particular nutrient. When an upper limit is also needed, then it is better that a range is given. Thus, the number and level of ingredients which could be included into a diet to give a DCP of 12·0 per cent exactly would be much less than those which would give a DCP of 12·0 per cent or above, or 12·0 to 12·5 per cent.

Further insistances as to minimum inclusion rates of particular ingredients can prove very restricting on a computer formulation. It is not just that this ingredient has to be included at the particular stated minimum level, but with that ingredient goes a particular balance of energy and amino acids and this balance influences the other ingredients which can be placed into the mix. Again, a maximum inclusion rate for a feedstuff which is currently advantageously priced can be expensive. The fewer the restraints, the more efficiently the program will run and the cheaper will be the final diet.

In practice, it is remarkably easy to restrain a least-cost computer programme into producing diets little different from the very simplest hand calculation, and no cheaper. Indeed, it is quite possible to produce an apparently innocent set of restraints which are mutually incompatable and no solution at all is obtainable. Occasionally, an unusual ingredient will be forced in at a very high price simply to adjust some imbalance of a minor amino acid or mineral. As a general rule therefore, all restraints, both of ingredients and nutrient specification, should be kept as few as possible, and based on hard evidence.

TABLE 11.5. Specification for a least-cost diet formulation for growing pigs, appropriate to a particular farm

Ingredients available:

Ingredient		Price	Restraint
Field beans	} home-grown	(£85)	at least 50 kg per tonne
Barley		(£55)	at least 200 kg per tonne
Wheat			no more than 200 kg per tonne
Maize			
Fish meal			
Ex. soya bean			
Wheat feed			no more than 100 kg per tonne
Di-calcium phosphate			
Vitamins and trace elements			exactly 3 kg per tonne
Total mix — 1 tonne			

Nutrient specification:

Digestible energy	12·9–13·1 MJ DE/kg
Digestible crude protein	13·5–14·0 per cent DCP
or crude protein	15·9–16·5 per cent CP
Lysine	at least 0·7 per cent
Methionine + cystine	at least 0·5 per cent
Calcium	at least 0·8 per cent
Phosphorus	at least 0·6 per cent

Notes: Field beans are 25 per cent CP. Some can be sold for £85 per tonne, but to use up a home-produced commodity they must be included at least at 5 per cent. The barley has 14 per cent moisture content and 10 per cent CP. All other ingredients purchased at current prices.

TABLE 11.6. Specification for a least-cost diet formulation for growing pigs appropriate to a small compounding mill

Ingredients available

All those listed in Appendix 2 at current market prices
Restraints on ingredients are noted in Appendix 2

Diet must contain at least 30 per cent barley and at least half of the supplementary protein must be soya bean

Total mix—5 tonne

Nutrient specification
As for Table 11.5.

Notes: Unless financially most attractive, the purchase of the following ingredients would rather be avoided: Sorghum, brewers' grain, roots (other than dried cooked potato), coconut, sunflower, microbial protein.

Setting up

Least-cost programs for pig diets are available from advisory services throughout the United Kingdom, the Scottish colleges, feed manufacturers, and a range of consultants. To use these services it is not necessary to be able to program a computer. However, many programs are contained in pre-written packages. Such packages may not always be the best for the particular circumstances of individual pig producers. In order to ensure that the best is obtained from a least-cost diet formulation service, the user may find it an advantage to prepare a list of requirements in longhand form.
1. The feedstuffs available, together with their nutritional values (or samples of the feedstuffs for chemical analysis).
2. Restraints in terms of minimum and maximum levels for each particular feed ingredient.
3. The diet specification for nutrient concentration (for example, as shown in Table 11.2).
4. The bulk of the final mix (usually the capacity of the mixer).
5. The current price for each of the potential ingredients (including handling, transport and storage costs).

In Table 11.5 is shown a specification which might be typical of a set of instructions for least-costing a pig-grower diet for a mixed farm. In Table 11.6 is given a similar specification but in this case as might

TABLE 11.7. Diet formulations from least-cost programs set up as indicated in Table 11.5. (mixed farm) and Table 11.6. (small compounding mill).

Ingredient	Price (£/tonne)	Quantity of ingredients (kg/tonne)	
		Farm	Mill
Barley	55	711	752
Wheat	60	118	79
Fish meal	135	74	21
Ex. soya bean	85	35	50
Dec. ground nut	90	—	50
Meat-and-bone meal	110	—	36
Field beans		50	
Salt	10	3·0	3·0
Calcium carbonate	11	6·0	5·5
Vitamin trace element mix	440	3·0	3·0
Price of mixed diet (£/tonne)		64·79	63·12

Prices (£/tonne) of ingredients not included: Oats 60; maize 70; flaked maize 75; wheat feed 60; di-calcium phosphate 125; molasses 55; tallow 200.

TABLE 11.8. Diet formulations from least-cost programs used at the Edinburgh School of Agriculture, solutions as at March 1975. (All values for ingredients are given in kg/tonne mix).

	Starter creep (4-28 days)			Standard creep (4 wks-40 kg)			Grower (40-70 kg)			Finisher (70 kg +)			Pregnant sow			Lactating sow		
	Min	Max	Final diet	Min	Max	Final diet	Min	Max	Final diet	Min	Max	Final diet	Min	Max	Final diet	Min	Max	Final diet
Ingredients																		
Barley		300	70		300	183		300	703		300	824		300	219		300	148
Wheat		250	250		250	250									300			300
Oats		100			100	89									47			161
Maize	200		200	100	100	100												
Flaked maize	50	75	64		100	100												
Wheat feed					30	63								400	400			
Fish meal		30	50		30	30			84			5						
Meat-and-bone meal			30					50			50			50			50	
Ex. soya bean			170			93		250	129		300	86					250	250
Ex. dec. cotton		0			0			50			50			50			50	
Ex. dec. ground nut		0			30	30		50	50		50	50		100	13		100	120
Skim milk	100		100															
Calcium carbonate						2			17			16						13
Di-calcium phosphate			13			4			11			13			15			2
Vitamins + trace elements	3	3	3	3	3	3	3	3	3	3	3	3	3	3	3	3	3	3
Salt		3	3		3	3		3	3		3	3		3	3		3	3
Molasses		50	50		50	50		50			50			50			50	
Tallow		50	50		50			50			50			50			50	
Nutrients																		
DE (MJ/kg)	13.7	14.3		13.5	14.0		12.5	13.0		12.5	13.0		11.8	12.4		12.5	13.0	
CP (%)	22.0	24.0		18.0	19.0		16.0	17.0		13.5	14.5		11.0	11.5		15.0	16.0	
DCP (%)	18.5	20.0		15.0	16.0		13.5	14.0		11.0	12.0		9.0	9.5		12.5	13.5	
Lysine (%)	1.1	1.3		.88	1.0		.69	.80		.60			.40	.60		.59	.70	
Meth + cyst (%)	.60	.70		.58	.70		.49	.65		.49			.40	.60		.45	.60	
Calcium (%)	.95	1.1		.90	1.0		.78	.81		.78	.81		.59	.61		.59	.61	
Phosphorus (%)	.85	.90		.78	.82		.59	.61		.59	.61		.49	.51		.49	.51	
Crude fibre (%)	1.0	3.0		2.0	4.0		2.0	5.0		2.0	6.0		2.0	7.0		2.0	6.0	
Ether extract (%)	1.0	5.0		1.0	5.0		1.0	6.0		1.0	6.0		1.0	5.0		1.0	5.0	

be appropriate to a small compounding mill. These specifications were put through the Edinburgh least-cost feed formulation program; the resultant diets are detailed in Table 11.7.

Some practical diets

In Table 11.8 is shown the ingredient and nutrient restraints together with final mixes for diets which have been used at the Edinburgh School of Agriculture. The computer program is run every month, and the ingredient formulations changed accordingly. As can be seen, the restraints imposed allow little change in creep diets, but the rules for the formulation of the pregnant sow and finishing pig diets are quite liberal. The energy density restraint changes in relation to appetite of the pig. Other restraints relate to the nutritional requirements of the pigs and a partially subjective view of which ingredients are appropriate for the various classes of pigs.

Frequent changes in diet ingredients

Where the inclusion into a diet of a new ingredient makes that diet less palatable, a change in diet ingredient could bring about a loss of production. Possibly of greater concern, is whether or not substitution of one palatable ingredient for another palatable ingredient may be deleterious simply because the pig reacts adversely to a change.

In general, there is no reason to suspect that pigs respond to feed ingredients rather than to nutrient specification. To a pig, 14 MJ of DE is 14 MJ DE whether it comes from 1 kg of wheat or 1·1 kg of barley. Further, most pigs are rationed to levels of intake below their appetite; the precise details of the type of cereal used is largely of academic interest to a hungry pig.

Problems could arise, however, with the sudden appearance of diet ingredients with unusual tastes or textures; fish meal, meat-and-bone meal and fine-ground wheat are examples. Another possible source of trouble might be with single-cereal diets; where a diet with 70 per cent or more of one cereal abruptly changes to being a diet with 70 per cent or more of a completely different cereal.

There can also be repercussions for pigs which are fed to appetite and which are being encouraged to eat as much as possible—sucking pigs, newly weaned pigs, young growers and lactating sows. These problems are usually avoided by the diet always containing a certain minimum proportion of a particular ingredient such as barley. Usually, the pig *does* respond to nutrient intake rather than the feedstuff which contains the nutrients.

THE DENSITY RESTRAINT AND UNIT VALUE OF NUTRIENTS

It has been argued that the pig's need is for a daily supply of particular quantities of nutrients; 24 MJ DE, 280 g DCP, etc. The daily requirements can be supplied by any number of different ration allowances, provided that the energy:protein ratio is maintained. In the present case, 24 MJ DE and 280 g DCP could be provided by 1·75 kg of a diet with 13·7 MJ DE/kg and 16 per cent DCP or 2·25 kg of a diet with 10·6 MJ DE/kg and 12·4 per cent DCP. If 2·25 kg is within the animal's appetite, the concentration of the nutrients does not matter, so long as the total daily nutrient needs for growth are satisfied. The difference between the diets is that the diet with 13·7 MJ DE/kg will be formulated mainly from energy-dense feedstuffs such as maize, wheat and perhaps a little fat (tallow or vegetable oil), whereas the diet with 10·6 MJ DE/kg will be formulated from low energy-dense feedstuffs such as wheat offals and oats.

So far, diets have been formulated within the restraint of a particular energy density which precludes particular feedstuffs, or limits their inclusion levels. This reduces price advantages which could be taken from the feedstuffs market.

The important characteristic of a feedstuff is not its price per unit weight, but its price per unit DE, per unit DCP, per unit lysine, etc. In Table 11·9 the unit values of nutrients in three feedstuffs are compared.

TABLE 11.9. Values of nutrients in three feedstuffs

	Barley	Wheat	Maize
Price (£/tonne):	55	60	61
DE (MJ/kg)	12·7	14·0	14·5
DCP (%)	7·7	8·3	7·3
Lysine (%)	·32	·28	·26
Cost (p):			
One MJ DE	0·43	0·43	0·42
One g DCP	·071	·072	·084
One g lysine	1·7	2·1	2·3

The cost, in pence, for 1 MJ DE, 1 g DCP and 1 g lysine is calculated on the basis of the whole of the feedstuff price being apportioned to each nutrient. This is, of course, not the case, but the values do serve for purposes of comparison, and to help decide which is the best buy. As these three cereals are often considered primarily as energy sources, the cost per unit energy would tend to be the most important; in this example maize would be selected.

However, in most pig diets at least half of the protein comes from the cereal fraction, so the cost per g protein and per g lysine has considerable importance. As maize contains low levels of these, the decision is a difficult one unless a complex sum is completed where the unit values for all three nutrients are compared *simultaneously*. Further the value that would be given to protein in grain depends upon the cost of protein in alternative protein sources. So to find out whether wheat, barley or maize is best buy, one needs to add soya bean into the set of equations for simultaneous solution. This is, of course, exactly what the least-cost linear program does; in fact it does rather better, simultaneously solving for 20 or more ingredients and for 10 or more nutrients.

On the supposition that the energy density restraint for a diet is set at 13 MJ DE/kg, and the price of maize falls further to £58/tonne, then despite the increased value of maize as an ingredient, only a limited amount of maize would be included because at 14·5 DE/kg it would take the diet beyond the 13 MJ restraint. Much of the financial advantage of maize would thereby be lost.

There are, therefore advantages to be gained from releasing the density restraint and instructing the computer to provide a diet which is formulated to least-cost provision of balanced nutrients. The program takes into account the fact that any change in energy density must be matched by a change in the density of all the other nutrients so that the ratios between the various nutrients remain stable. The program also allows for the fact if the diet is less dense more of it must be fed; or conversely, less fed if the diet is more dense, to provide the same daily nutrients.

In Table 11.10 the problem is to supply one day's nutrient need to a pig at least cost. Two pricing situations are shown which may readily occur over a six-month period—in the first situation the high density diet is best, in the second the low density diet is best.

TABLE 11.10. Value of three diets

Diet	Cost (£/tonne)	Ration (kg) to provide 24 MJ DE and 280 g DCP	Cost (p) to provide one day's nutrient requirements
A. High density	75	1·8	13·5
B. Medium density	72	2	14·4
C. Low density	66	2·2	14·5
A. High density	80	1·8	14·4
B. Medium density	70	2	14·0
C. Low density	62	2·2	13·6

In practice the density restraint *is* invoked, and very often stipulated as an exact value (13·0 MJ DE/kg, for example). There are valid reasons for this, although real savings in feed costs per unit of pig growth may be lost.

Probably the most rigidly adhered to of all policies on a pig unit is the rationing policy. Advice may even be given in terms of rations. Thus, 'Pregnant sows are to get 2 kg (4½ lb)/day, lactating sows 4 kg (9 lb) for the sow and 0·4 kg (1 lb) for every pig over 5, fatteners are fed to a scale which does not go above 2·5 kg (5½ lb) daily,' and so on. Such statements are valueless when quoted independently of the nutrient concentrations of the diets which are to be rationed; the pigs require quantities of this or that *nutrient* daily, not quantities of feed. There is a certain safety in having all pig diets of a standard energy density (usually 12·5–13 MJ DE/kg).

There are other problems when it comes to feeding management. Particular rationing regimes are familiar to the feeder, and these may even be an integral part of a recording system. There is plenty of scope for confusion where a change in nutrient density can require a reduction in the daily ration to effect an increase in nutrient supply.

Nevertheless, the benefits which can accrue warrant that more attention is given to this most effective means of keeping down the cost of pig diets.

High nutrient density diets

The popularity of high nutrient density diets (above 13·5 MJ DE/kg) varies in relation to the unit price of energy in energy-dense feedstuffs. As maize, wheat, soya beans and fat pre-mixes decrease in price in relation to barley and wheat offals, high density diets become more advantageous with respect to the price which has to be paid for each unit of pig growth. If the pig eats *nutrients,* then the concentration of the diet is of no concern to it and there is nothing to be gained or lost because a diet is more or less dense. However, high nutrient density does, of itself, have three intrinsic advantages.

Sucking pigs and growers often gain in liveweight more slowly than they need, simply because they cannot eat enough. Their stomach capacity does not allow the intake of sufficient nutrients to satisfy the maximum rate of protein deposition together with the appropriate rate of fat growth. These young animals need diets of the highest nutrient density compatible with palatability. If the growing pig is not yet up to its maximum rate of protein deposition, then its use of a further increment of feed will be primarily in lean tissue growth. To pay a premium can therefore be justified for a quality, energy-dense, protein-dense diet specially formulated for this class of pig.

The second advantage of the high density diet is that the type of feedstuffs used (particularly maize, wheat and soya bean) are of consistent quality and predictable in the way the pig responds to them. Conversely, feedstuffs of low nutrient density (oats, grass meal, miller's offals, etc) tend to be unpredictable. High density diets can therefore be formulated more precisely.

The third advantage of the high density diet is the saving in transport and handling costs. These savings are achieved as a result of the same weight of diet carrying more nutrients in it. Cost saving starts at the mill, continues through storage and haulage, and is also achieved by the producer who has to get the feed into the pig's pen and the slurry out of it.

To use a high nutrient density diet is to allow the pig to eat more. Where the pig's appetite allows a rate of consumption greater than the daily nutrient allowance, the feed scales should be reduced strictly in accord with the increase in nutrient density. Because the diet is denser, less of it will be fed for each unit of weight gained, so the feed conversion efficiency will improve. Energetic efficiency will remain the same. The vital question is not the efficiency of conversion of food or energy, but the cost per unit of pig growth. On a low density diet, it is possible for growth to be obtained cheaply while the feed conversion efficiency is very poor.

HOW MANY DIETS?

A different diet is needed if a change in the ratio of nutrients is required; particularly a change in energy:protein ratio or in amino acid balance. Different diets are also indicated where appetite considerations call for low or high nutrient density, or particular qualities of texture or palatability. Lastly, special diet ingredients appropriate only to specific circumstances may be necessary. Some characteristics for diets have been identified in Table 11.11 (page 172).

Table 11.11 gives six classes of pigs as requiring different diets, the 'grower' class, however, covers a wide range of energy:protein ratios (1:9–1:13), so there are a further three or so diets within this class. As the pig grows, the energy demand for purposes of maintenance and fat production increase, but because the rate of protein deposition is fairly constant over the growth phase the demand for protein increases less (only to balance the requirements of protein maintenance). Thus there is a smooth decline in the required energy:protein ratio as the animal grows. The actual quantity of protein needed daily increases, but not nearly as fast as the increase in energy.

The spectre of numerous diets is not so alarming if automatic mixing and feeding facilities are on hand; when a flick of a switch changes the energy:protein ratio. But in all other circumstances the

TABLE 11.11. Diet characteristics for six classes of pigs

	Pregnant sow	Lactating sow	Starter creep	Standard creep and weaner	Grower (40-70 kg)	Finisher (70 kg +)
Energy: protein ratio (MJ DE: g DCP)	1:8	1:10	1:15	1:13-15	1:9-13	1:8-10
Energy density of diet (MJ DE/kg)	<13	13	14	13·5-14	13-14	12-13
Biological value of protein	60-70	65-70	70-80	70-75	70	65
Appetite factors	— —	+	+++	+++		—
Special ingredients[1]			++	+		
Additives: bacteriostats			+	+	+	
growth promoters			+	+	+	

[1] special ingredients usually in form of dried milk, whey, cooked oats, flaked maize, vegetable fats, sugar, salt, spices etc.

answer to the question, 'How many diets?' must be, 'As few as possible'. The lowest possible number is one.

If special creep diets are not fed, if protein is overfed to the pregnant sows, if finishing pigs are provided with rather too sophisticated a diet and if less than maximum growth is accepted in the weaners; then a single diet for all pigs is possible. The most appropriate would be one similar to that for lactating sows.

Simplification

Although six diets are shown in Table 11.8, reference to Table 11.11 suggests that some contraction might be possible in many circumstances with little loss of efficiency. There are two extreme classes of diets: low quality (pregnant sow and finisher) and high quality (creep feeds). In the middle are the lactating sow and grower diets. Some additives are absent from adult sow diets.

If the starter creep mix is abandoned, a three-diet system is possible—particularly if the strain of pig is a lean one which has a high daily rate of protein deposition and which can use high protein:high energy diets. Standard creep and weaner is fed from three weeks until 60 kg or so. The lactating sow diet is formulated to have a little less protein (energy:protein ratio of 1:9) and is also fed to the finishing pigs. This combination allows considerable freedom in the formulation of a cheap pregnant sow diet. Other combinations will be appropriate for different circumstances.

Formulating diets with bulky feedstuffs

Some useful feeds for pigs are not readily incorporated into a conventional dry concentrate diet. The bulky nature of these feedstuffs is usually resultant from a high content of fibre or of water.

Nutritionally, there is no reason for such feeds to be treated differently from any others; although it is more difficult to obtain reliable nutritive evaluation. Where nutritive value varies with stage of growth, as for example with grass, adjustments must be made to DE and DCP levels attributed to the feedstuff. Similarly, for feeds high in water it has to be recognised that most of the ingested diet will have no nutritive value. A relatively constant water content as may be found in skimmed milk or whey is less of a problem than a water content which varies, as is the case with some brewers' grains, potatoes and root crops. A small change in water content brings about large changes in nutritional value.

Given the correct nutritive value of the feedstuff, it may be formulated into a diet in the prescribed way. Wet-feed ingredients can readily be incorporated into pipe-line or river-feeding systems, which are ideal for coping with skim milk, whey, macerated root crops, liquified fish and so on. The bulky feed component need not, however, always be *physically mixed* with the other ingredients in the diet formulation. The non-bulky part of the diet can be fed separately in the form of a balancer meal. This meal is formulated to match the bulky ingredient and will be protein-rich for bulky energy sources, and energy-rich for bulky protein sources.

In some cases an energy source may, by nature of its bulk or unpalatability, self-limit its intake. In this event, diet formulation may simply comprise the provision of a set quantity of a protein-rich balancer diet, together with free access to the energy source. For sows, an estimate is made of the intake of the bulky feedstuff and the ration of balancer meal adjusted to the requirement for pregnancy or lactation. For growing pigs, the appetite increases with age and weight, and so therefore does the intake of the bulky part of the diet. Because the intake of the protein-rich balancer is rationed to a set amount, the energy:protein ratio widens as the pig grows. If the energy source contains 6 to 8 per cent DCP (as would often be the case), the rate at which the energy:protein ratio changes conveniently approximates to the requirement.

Compensatory protein growth

The single diet pig unit is too attractive a proposition to be discarded without careful examination. At the moment, advocates of a single diet appear to be in two camps: (1) commercial farmers who know better than always to do what nutritionists suggest, and (2) nutritionists who have the virtue of unconventionality. In the latter camp is a group of Polish workers, whose ideas, although unsubstantiated, are worthy of consideration. The Polish philosophy depends upon the existence of compensatory growth.

Weaners up to 30 kg (65 lb) liveweight are deliberately rationed. In UK, normal practice is to *ad lib* feed to obtain maximum growth at this time when the pig is growing lean. Rationing slows down growth but also reduces, it is claimed, enteric disorders. From 30 kg, the pigs are fed the diet (of about 15–16 per cent CP) at the rate of 2 kg/day for 30 days. For the second term of 30 days 2·5 kg is fed, and for the third term 3·0 kg. After 90 days of feeding the pigs should weigh about 100 kg. It is accepted by the Polish group that for the first 45 days the pigs are underfed protein and for the last 45 days they are overfed protein. The assumption is that during the time they are overfed, the pigs will gain extra amounts of protein daily to compensate for the lost protein growth when they were underfed.

Controversy usually rages where objective evidence is short and this is certainly the case for compensatory growth. If the pig *can* make compensatory growth in lean tissue, feeding could be considerably simplified; the rule being that whilst the pig must get his total allowance sometime in a 100-day growth period, the apportionment of that allowance is not critical. On the other hand, if compensatory protein growth is not sufficient to fully make up previous losses, failure to correctly apportion the dietary protein will lead to inefficient feeding. At present, where hard evidence is lacking it is probably wisest to err on the side of caution.

The weaner pig

Prior to 14–21 days of age the digestive system of the piglet is prepared to deal with milk-protein and milk-energy. After this age the piglet can cope with non-milk nutrient sources to an ever increasing degree. Formulating diets for the piglet of less than 14 days of age is primarily a matter of providing milk in a form that is readily consumed. After 14 days, formulation centres around palatability rather than nutritional considerations. Some specially palatable ingredients are listed in the footnote to Table 11.11 (page 172).

As there is a chance that pigs weaned before 21–28 days of age will die, medicaments are also an important component of early-weaner diets. The stress placed on palatability for weaner diets allows for a fair number of secret ingredients. Amongst these have been sugar, dates, coal, barley-sprouts, honey and sugar-coated expanded wheat, hot water, alcohol and tinned pilchards. With regret, it must be reported that diets based on conventional ingredients have been found quite satisfactory. A specification for the 21-day early weaner diet would therefore be rather similar to that for the starter creep. The younger the pig, the higher should be the inclusion of milk powder and the more stress laid on palatability.

NON-NUTRITIONAL FEED ADDITIVES FOR GROWTH PROMOTION

Feed additives may serve purposes of:
1. Improving palatability.
2. Improving texture of meals and physical characteristics of pellets (hardness or softness).
3. Prevention of rancidity (oxidation of fats) and preservation of vitamin potency.
4. Curing infections, particularly bacterial and parasitic infections of the digestive tract.
5. Preventing infections.
6. Promotion of growth.

The distinction between preventing infection and promoting growth is often subtle.

Feed antibiotics and antibacterial agents

The antibiotics have been divided into two groups, those for therapeutic use and those for growth promotion. These groups are mutually exclusive. The action of antibiotics in promoting growth is not completely understood, but they control micro-organisms in the alimentary tract. Currently in use are such materials as virginiamycin, moenomycin and zinc bacitracin. Other chemical compounds which have bacteriostatic, and possibly other properties, can, although do not invariably, promote growth without harmful side effects or tissue residues. This group includes nitrosin, quindoxin, dimetridazole and halquinol. Although successful as a growth promoter, quindoxin has been withdrawn and is no longer available.

Antibiotics and antibacterial agents in the therapeutic list may be obtained on prescription from veterinary surgeons. These agents control overt disease symptoms as well as promoting growth. Conditions in some units are such that without continual additions of therapeutic antibiotics into the feed, performance would be markedly reduced. Examples in this group are sulphonamides, penicillin, tylosin, nitrofurazone, furazolidone, tetracyclines.

Copper and arsenicals

Levels of copper above 200 g/tonne used to be included, but now a level of 175 g/tonne is recommended. The European Economic Community permitted maximum is 125 g/tonne. There has been some evidence of copper residues in pig livers and also in soils treated with pig slurry. The growth-promoting effects of dietary copper seem to be additive to the effects of other growth promoters.

For growth promotion by use of arsenical compounds, up to 100 g/tonne may be included into growing pig diets. Residues may be found in tissues, but they disappear rapidly when ingestion of the arsenical compound stops. For this reason feeds containing arsenic must not be given to pigs within 10 days of slaughter.

The actions of copper and arsenic compounds are still improperly known, but both seem to have some selective effect upon the microbial population of the alimentary tract.

Hormones

Hormone implants have been used in bovines for a number of years. In the past, however, administration of hormones to growing pigs has often produced negative results or no effect. More recently, a combination of synthetic androgen (methyltestosterone) and a synthetic oestrogen (diethylstilboestrol) has achieved some success in the promotion of growth. The mixture has some anabolic activity which increases the rate of protein synthesis. Enhanced protein synthesis further results in improved efficiency of food use and a reduction in fatness.

The hormone mixture may affect reproductive performance, the additive is therefore not recommended for diets fed to potential breeding stock. It is further recommended that pigs are not fed supplemented diets in the 72 hours prior to slaughter. It would appear that the administration of the material has an effect similar to a small increase in the maximum daily rate of protein deposition. As there is no evidence of an enhanced efficiency of protein use, the dietary protein supply should be commensurate with the greater daily rate of deposition.

Response
Most additives can, but do not always, give a 3–8 per cent improvement in efficiency of feed use and rate of liveweight gain. A common feature is that responses are usually *variable* both between pig units and within pig units between time periods. Responses tend to be greatest where the system is inadequate; for example, where there is a high disease risk, housing is below standard, stock is of poor strain and the management input low. Feed additives increase the cost of a diet and their inclusion will only be cost effective if (a) the improved performance covers the cost of the additive, and (b) the same improvement could not be gained by less expensive means; perhaps by a change in the management system, or use of an improved strain of pig.

It has yet to be proven that feed additives achieve any response over and above that obtained by the solution of the problem which requires their use. In view of the uncertainty regarding modes of action of many additives, it would appear to be only reasonable to resolve such troubles as are caused by sub-clinical infections, etc, rather than cover them up with an additive.

Chapter 12

IN CONCLUSION

THE CONCLUSION of the text represents the view, ever more widely held by producers and compounders, that a change in direction is under way in the field of pig nutrition.

The movement is away from the 'National Plan' approach involving generalised recommendations, and towards the acceptance of the philosophy of greater freedom of choice. If individual producers are to maximise their profits, diets and feeding programs must relate to the particular circumstances of individual producers.

Freedom of choice for the producers does not remove the responsibility of the nutritionist, rather responsibility is increased. Again, the acceptance that there are differences between pigs in their responses to dietary nutrients increases the need to quantify the effects of feeding on pig growth and reproduction in strict numerical terms, rather than in generalisations.

SOME SPECIFIC POINTS

Individualism

The individualistic nature of pigs, of each pig producer's circumstances, and of the market forces existing at any one moment in time, means that although nutritional information must be exact, it must also be used flexibly. This being the case, the methods for solving the problem of how to optimise the production process is *bound to be complicated;* but the solutions produced by these calculations can be very *simple*, as can their implementation.

Nutritional abuses

Pigs can tolerate some abuses, but not others. Where there is an energy need, fat can be used as an energy buffer, both for growing pigs and sows. In the case of protein and many of the other nutrients, the existence of compensating mechanisms are more doubtful and yet unresolved. Failure to provide for the optimum daily nutrient requirements in these cases may lead to irretrievable loss of production.

IN CONCLUSION

Using models

It has been suggested that the solution to some nutritional problems can be most readily approached by use of the technique of modelling. At present, research in this area is active and modelling is becoming more widely used in field situations. It is a characteristic of the modelling approach that the answers obtained cannot be expressed in a generalised form. Neither can the mathematics be described or simplified such that individuals could build their own models. For modelling to work well, there must be a direct link between the individual producer and the computer. Because the inputs for models rely on the specific circumstances of individuals, the output is also specific and cannot be used as a ready solution for other circumstances.

Husbandry practices

Some nutritional practices stem from adherence to tradition rather than logic. Where no information is available, common husbandry practice is the best place to start from. But progress is made by re-examining the rules and altering them where necessary, not by adhering unquestioningly to tradition. In many cases 'husbandry laws' are found to be no longer applicable in circumstances where they are still used.

Problem variables in the pig

There are two variables in particular which are vital to pig-feeding but have received scant attention. The first relates to the dominant rôle of the nutritional demands of the lactation in influencing weight losses from the sow, and thereby the feeding program required. The second concerns the presence (or absence) of an inherent maximum to the daily rate of protein (lean) growth that can be made by growing pigs and which appears to differ between sex and genetic strain of pig. This maximum colours the whole spectrum of nutritional decisions, but can only yet be roughly approximated.

Problem variables in the feed

The ideal balance of amino acids in protein for feeding to both growing and breeding pigs is imperfectly known. Until more information comes forward, the various amino acid mixtures available from protein in feedstuffs cannot be combined together in such a way as to optimise protein use in monetary terms.

With regard to energy, two questions are of particular significance. What is the effective energy supply from feedstuffs high in fibre or high in fat; and does this energy supply alter with the level of dietary inclusion of these feeds? Until these are answered the use of diets of particularly high or low nutrient density will be circumscribed—to the detriment of efficient feedstuff usage.

Body weight

The weight measurement of the pig has one particular attribute; it is an easy quantitative measurement to take. For this reason alone it is of great potential use. But the body weight of the pig does not say anything about the proportions of lean and fat, about the potential of the pig for further growth, or about its reproductive capability. For sows, weight without knowledge of age, size, fatness and condition is of limited use as a means of monitoring productivity or for selecting an appropriate feeding program. For growing pigs it is worth considering that weight adds little information that could be used for feeding strategy which would not be provided by a measurement of time; and the number of days a pig has been in the fattening house is an even easier measurement to take than liveweight.

In conclusion

Although dependent upon the written word, we have attempted to describe aspects of nutrition upon which practical action could be taken; to suggest to nutritionist and producer that pig growth and reproductive capacity is under the direct control of the feeder, and open to exploitation by active manipulation.

We are well aware, as are producers and compounders, that the state of nutritional knowledge is very inadequate and insufficient to allow the degree of control of pig productivity that would be wished for. However, this does not detract from the objective, and the information needed is coming forward continually.

APPENDICES

APPENDIX 1. Metabolic body weights ($W^{0.75}$)

Weight of pig (kg)	Metabolic body weight (kg)	Weight of pig (kg)	Metabolic body weight (kg)	Weight of pig (kg)	Metabolic body weight (kg)	Weight of pig (kg)	Metabolic body weight (kg)	Weight of pig (kg)	Metabolic body weight (kg)
1	1·00	23	10·5	45	17·4	67	23·4	89	29·0	155	43·9
2	1·68	24	10·8	46	17·7	68	23·7	90	29·2	160	44·9
3	2·28	25	11·2	47	18·0	69	23·9	91	29·4	165	45·9
4	2·83	26	11·5	48	18·2	70	24·2	92	29·7	170	47·0
5	3·34	27	11·8	49	18·5	71	24·4	93	29·9	175	48·1
6	3·83	28	12·2	50	18·8	72	24·7	94	30·2	180	49·1
7	4·30	29	12·5	51	19·1	73	25·0	95	30·4	185	50·1
8	4·75	30	12·8	52	19·4	74	25·2	96	30·7	190	51·2
9	5·19	31	13·1	53	19·6	75	25·5	97	30·9	200	53·2
10	5·62	32	13·5	54	19·9	76	25·8	98	31·1	210	55·2
11	6·04	33	13·8	55	20·2	77	26·0	99	31·4	220	57·2
12	6·44	34	14·1	56	20·5	78	26·2	100	31·6	230	59·1
13	6·84	35	14·4	57	20·8	79	26·5	105	32·8	240	61·0
14	7·24	36	14·7	58	21·0	80	26·7	110	34·0	250	62·8
15	7·62	37	15·0	59	21·3	81	27·0	115	35·1	260	64·7
16	8·00	38	15·3	60	21·6	82	27·2	120	36·2	270	66·6
17	8·38	39	15·6	61	21·8	83	27·5	125	37·4	280	68·4
18	8·75	40	15·9	62	22·1	84	27·7	130	38·5	290	70·3
19	9·10	41	16·2	63	22·4	85	28·0	135	39·6	300	72·1
20	9·46	42	16·5	64	22·6	86	28·2	140	40·7	350	80·9
21	9·8	43	16·8	65	22·9	87	28·5	145	41·8	400	89·4
22	10·2	44	17·1	66	23·2	88	28·7	150	42·8	500	105·7

APPENDIX II

APPENDIX 2. Guide to nutritive values of some feeds (expressed on the basis of fresh material fed at the dry matter indicated)

	Dry matter (%)	Crude fibre (%)	Ether extract (fat) (%)	Gross energy (MJ GE/kg)	Digestibility (% of GE)	Digestible energy (MJ DE/kg)	Protein (%CP, N × 6.25)	Digestibility (% of protein)	Digestible protein (% DCP)	Nitrogen-free DE (MJ DE/kg)	Lysine (%)	Threonine (%)	Methionine + cystine (%)	Calcium (%)	Phosphorus (%)	Protein quality value (BV)	
Cereals																	
Barley	86	4.8	1.5	16.0	79	12.7	10.0	77	7.7	10.8	0.32	0.35	0.27	0.04	0.33	46	– Often included at a minimum of 25% to maintain continuity in diet mixtures
Wheat	86	3.0	1.7	16.2	86	14.0	10.3	81	8.3	12.0	0.28	0.32	0.38	0.03	0.34	43	– Avoid fine grinding; sometimes limited to a maximum of 50% in the diet
Oats	86	10.0	4.2	16.9	67	11.4	10.3	75	7.7	9.6	0.37	0.35	0.40	0.07	0.32	59	
Maize	86	2.0	3.6	16.2	90	14.5	8.6	85	7.3	12.8	0.26	0.35	0.25	0.02	0.24	50	– When cooked, DE is raised by about 3% and DCP reduced by about 3%
Sorghum	86	2.3	3.7	15.9	90	14.3	9.5	76	7.3	12.6	0.23	0.32	0.34	0.03	0.29	34	
Brewers' grains	90	15.0	6.4	16.5	46	7.6	18.0	75	13.5	4.4	0.74	–	–	0.29	0.70	–	⎧ The effects of inclusions of quantities of brewer's and miller's offals with a high fibre content are largely unknown. In particular
Fine wheat middlings	88	8.0	4.0	16.9	70	11.9	15.5	64	9.9	9.6	0.64	0.48	0.54	0.14	0.74	59	⎨ there is a possible effect on the overall digestibility of dietary energy and protein.
Bran	88	13.0	4.0	16.5	50	8.3	15.0	40	6.0	6.5	0.60	0.40	0.47	0.20	2.50	31	⎩ Often limited to a maximum of 25% of the diet
Others																	
Cassava	90	3.7	0.5	15.4	92	14.2	3.2	41	1.3	13.9	0.11	0.07	0.05	–	–	33	– Contains glucosides, largely removed by grinding and drying
Swede turnips	12	1.2	0.2	2.0	85	1.7	1.5	60	0.9	1.5	0.05	–	0.02	0.05	0.04	–	⎧ High water content may limit intake if included at high levels. Root crops are
Fodder beet	22	1.3	0.1	3.4	85	2.9	1.5	47	0.7	2.7	0.04	0.04	0.02	0.04	0.04	–	⎨ potential diet ingredients where a wet feeding system is used
Potato–cooked	90	2.0	0.4	15.5	93	14.4	9.1	84	7.6	12.6	0.48	0.35	0.18	0.08	0.16	67	– Of similar value to maize; increases the hardness of pellets. Highly digestible
Potato–raw	20	0.4	0.1	3.4	68	2.3	2.4	19	0.5	2.2	0.13	0.09	0.05	0.02	0.04	–	– Contains high levels of trypsin inhibitor; disliked by pigs
Grass meal	90	17.3	3.0	15.2	39	5.9	15.0	33	5.0	4.7	0.90	0.60	0.50	0.86	0.30	66	– Usually limited to 5–10% rate of inclusion, which increases DE and palatability
Fat and oil	98	–	98.0	34.0	85	29.0	–	–	–	29.0	–	–	–	–	–	–	– DE value may vary widely between sources.

184 PRACTICAL PIG NUTRITION

APPENDIX 2. (Contd.) Guide to nutritive values of some feeds (expressed on the basis of fresh material fed at the dry matter indicated)

	Dry matter (%)	Crude fibre (%)	Ether extract (fat) (%)	Gross energy (MJ GE/kg)	Digestibility (% of GE)	Digestible energy (MJ DE/kg)	Protein (% CP, N × 6.25)	Digestibility (% of protein)	Digestible protein (% DCP)	Nitrogen-free DE (MJ DE/kg)	Lysine (%)	Threonine (%)	Methionine + cystine (%)	Calcium (%)	Phosphorus (%)	Protein quality value (BV)	
Protein feeds																	
White fish meal	90	—	4·0	17·8	85	15·1	62	93	58	1·4	4·6	2·9	2·5	7·1	3·7	77	– Some heat damage to protein possible
Herring meal	90	—	8·0	18·9	92	17·4	69	94	65	2·1	5·1	3·2	2·6	2·9	2·2	77	– Needs to be de-oiled; high oil may taint the carcass fat
Meat-and-bone meal	90	—	8·0	14·5	54	7·8	50	65	33	—	3·3	1·7	1·2	10·3	5·4	60	– Can be a variable product; often limited to a maximum of 5% in the diet
Skim milk	90	—	0·5	17·0	97	16·5	32	100	32	8·9	2·2	1·4	1·1	1·0	0·8	83	
SCP 1	90	—	1·0	20·4	85	17·2	59	91	54	5·7	4·2	2·6	1·5	0·1	1·4	63	⎧ Single cell protein (SCP) sources have yet
SCP 2	90	—	—	20·0	85	17·0	73	91	66	2·8	4·4	3·2	2·1	0·2	2·2	67	⎨ to be comprehensively tested. These two products exemplify the potential of SCP
Ex. soya bean	90	4·3	1·5	17·6	85	15·0	45	90	41	5·3	2·8	1·9	1·3	0·3	0·7	86	– Can contain trypsin inhibitor if imperfectly heat treated. Some heat damage also possible
Ex. rape seed	90	13·7	2·6	—	—	12·2	36	86	31	4·9	1·8	1·6	1·5	0·7	1·0	63	– Contains thioglucosides; often limited to a maximum of 3% in the diet
Ex. dec. ground nut	90	5·9	0·7	18·7	75	14·0	49	90	44	3·5	1·8	1·3	1·4	0·1	0·6	51	– Can contain aflatoxins; often limited to a maximum of 3% in the diet
Field beans	86	5·9	1·3	16·2	78	12·6	26	78	20	7·9	1·6	0·9	0·4	0·1	0·6	53	– Low level of trypsin inhibitor; often limited to provide no more than half supplementary protein
Ex. cotton seed	90	12·0	6·0	17·2	64	11·0	41	70	29	3·0	1·6	1·4	1·4	0·3	1·3	60	– Contains gossypols; often limited to a maximum of 3% in the diet
Ex. sunflower	90	12·0	2·3	—	—	12·6	38	82	31	5·3	1·6	1·6	1·5	0·4	1·2	60	– Often limited to 3% in the diet
Ex. coconut	90	13·0	7·5	—	—	13·6	20	70	14	10·3	0·6	0·7	0·7	0·4	0·7	43	– Possibility of unidentified toxic factors; usually limited to about 3% in the diet
Ca and P supplements																	
Steamed bone flour	98	—	—	—	—	—	—	—	—	—	—	—	—	40·0	14·0	—	
Dicalcium phosphate	100	—	—	—	—	—	—	—	—	—	—	—	—	22·0	18·0	—	
Calcium carbonate	100	—	—	—	—	—	—	—	—	—	—	—	—	33·0	—	—	

APPENDIX III

APPENDIX 3. Amino acid composition of the protein in feedstuffs (g/16g N or % amino acid in protein)*

	Whole egg	Barley	Wheat	Oats	Maize	Sorghum	Rice	Wheat middlings	Bran	Fodder beet	Potato	Grass	Cassava	Meat and bone	Fish meal	Skim milk	SCP 1	SCP 2	Ex. soya bean	Ex. rape seed	Ex. cotton seed	Ex. dec. groundnut	Ex. sunflower seed	Ex. coconut	Field beans	Pig
Arginine	6.6	5.5	4.7	8.0	4.5	4.0	6.5	6.0	3.9	2.4	5.6	5.8	10.0	7.5	5.6	3.2	4.9	4.5	7.2	5.7	11.0	11.1	9.5	11.2	8.0	—
Histidine	2.4	2.1	2.2	1.6	2.5	2.3	3.0	2.6	2.0	1.2	2.2	2.0	1.0	1.8	2.3	2.5	1.9	2.0	2.6	2.4	2.7	2.3	2.7	1.7	2.4	2.5
Isoleucine	6.6	4.9	5.3	5.1	3.8	3.8	4.5	3.4	4.2	1.6	3.2	3.3	2.0	3.4	4.9	7.0	4.3	4.4	5.0	3.6	4.0	3.6	4.5	4.0	3.8	4.0
Leucine	8.8	6.1	6.5	7.7	11.8	9.7	6.2	5.8	7.1	2.3	4.8	10.2	3.5	6.4	7.6	9.8	7.0	6.8	7.6	5.8	6.2	6.2	7.3	6.0	6.9	8.0
Lysine	6.4	3.2	3.0	4.1	2.7	2.4	4.0	4.1	2.2	2.3	5.3	6.0	3.5	6.6	7.4	7.0	7.2	6.3	6.2	5.0	4.2	3.6	4.2	3.0	6.0	7.0
Methionine	3.1	1.8	2.0	1.7	1.8	1.7	2.3	1.5	1.6	—	1.1	2.1	1.0	1.4	2.9	2.2	1.5	2.5	1.4	1.7	1.5	1.1	2.2	1.6	0.6	2.0
Phenylalanine	5.8	5.8	4.5	6.0	4.0	4.7	4.0	4.2	4.7	1.4	3.6	8.8	2.0	3.5	4.4	4.2	3.9	3.5	5.0	3.5	5.3	5.2	5.3	4.2	4.0	4.0
Threonine	5.0	3.5	3.0	3.7	3.8	3.9	3.5	3.1	2.9	2.4	3.9	4.0	2.1	3.4	4.6	4.5	4.4	4.6	4.2	4.4	3.3	2.6	4.1	3.7	3.5	4.0
Tryptophan	1.7	1.4	1.0	1.3	0.5	1.3	1.5	1.3	1.6	—	1.1	2.1	0.5	0.7	1.4	1.3	1.3	1.0	1.4	1.5	1.6	0.8	1.3	0.9	0.8	1.0
Tyrosine	4.3	3.5	3.0	4.0	3.9	3.3	5.1	3.1	1.1	2.2	3.4	3.1	1.6	2.4	3.5	2.9	4.0	3.1	3.6	2.7	3.2	4.2	2.8	2.4	3.3	3.0
Valine	7.4	5.0	4.4	5.7	4.5	5.5	6.0	4.9	4.5	2.3	4.3	10.6	2.6	4.9	5.6	7.9	5.3	5.3	5.0	4.7	5.0	4.2	5.9	5.5	4.3	5.5
Cystine	2.3	1.8	2.0	2.3	2.0	2.2	1.5	2.2	1.5	0.6	0.9	1.1	0.6	0.9	1.1	1.1	0.9	0.6	1.4	2.4	1.7	1.4	1.7	1.9	1.0	1.0

Sources of information for Appendices 2 and 3, N.A.S.–N.R.C. 1968. *Nutrient Requirements of Swine*. Publication No. 1599. Washington.
Peers, D. G. 1974. *Typical Nutritive Values of Feedingstuffs*. Internal publ. Edinburgh School of Agriculture.
Evans, R. E. 1960. *Bulletin No. 48*. M.A.F.F., H.M.S.O., London.
Pond, W. G. and Maner, J. H. 1974. *Swine Production in Temperate and Tropical Environments*. W. H. Freeman & Co., San Francisco.
Mitchell, H. H. 1964. *Comparative Nutrition of Man and Domestic Animals*. Academic Press, London.
Bolton, W. 1967. *Bulletin No. 174*. M.A.F.F., H.M.S.O., London.
Harvey, D. 1970. *Technical Communication No. 19*. Commonwealth Agricultural Bureau, Farnham Royal, England.
Morgan, D. J., Cole, D. J. A. and Lewis, D. 1975. *J. agric. Sci., Camb.* **84**, 7.

*Can be converted to amino acid composition of feedstuff by multiplying value by percentage protein in the feedstuff.

APPENDIX 4. Some conversions—imperial to metric measurements

For diet formulation

1 lb = 454 g = 0·454 kg
1 ton ⁓ 1 tonne
1 part per million (ppm) = 1 mg/kg = 1 g/tonne
1 lb/ton = 0·446 kg/tonne = 0·045%
1% = 22·4 lb/ton = 10 kg/tonne
7 lb/ton ⁓ 3 kg/tonne
5 lb/ton ⁓ 2·25 kg/tonne

14 lb ⁓ 6·25 kg	10 lb ⁓ 4·5 kg
28 lb ⁓ 12·5 kg	20 lb ⁓ 9 kg
56 lb ⁓ 25 kg	30 lb ⁓ 13·5 kg
112 lb ⁓ 50 kg	40 lb ⁓ 18 kg
5 cwt ⁓ 250 kg	50 lb ⁓ 23 kg
10 cwt ⁓ 500 kg	140 lb ⁓ 64 kg

1300 k cals/lb = 2850 k cals/kg = 12 MJ/kg
1400 k cals/lb = 3100 k cals/kg = 13 MJ/kg
1500 k cals/lb = 3450 k cals/kg = 14 MJ/kg

1 kg of an average cereal-based pig diet contains about:
 0·70 starch equivalent (SE)
 0·70 total digestible nutrients (TDN)
 3·1 Mcals digestible energy (DE)
 13 MJ DE
 12·5 MJ metabolisable energy (ME)
 9·0 MJ net energy (NE)

Pig weights

 2·0 lb ⁓ 0·9 kg, 2·5 lb ⁓ 1·1 kg, 3·0 lb ⁓ 1·4 kg
 12 lb ⁓ 5 kg, 22 lb ⁓ 10 kg, 35 lb ⁓ 16 kg
 45 lb ⁓ 20 kg, 120 lb ⁓ 55 kg, 155 lb ⁓ 70 kg, 200 lb ⁓ 91 kg
 220 lb ⁓ 100 kg, 250 lb ⁓ 115 kg, 300 lb ⁓ 140 kg, 400 lb ⁓ 180 kg

House temperatures

 86°F hot 30°C
 68°F warm 20°C
 59°F cool 15°C
 50°F cold 10°C

INDEX

INDEX

Additives, 175
Amino acids, 39
—, availability, 43
—, balance, 44
—, essential, 40
—, in feedstuffs, 183, 184
—, in pigmeat, 45, 185
—, in proteins, 49, 185
—, non-essential, 48
—, supplementation, 47
Antibiotics, 176
Appetite, 88
—, growing pigs, 88, 171, 175
—, sows, 91, 101
Arsenicals, 176

Biological value, 50
—, of diet, 120, 158
—, of feedstuffs, 183, 184
Boar, 24
—, fertility, 27, 30
—, rationing, 140
Bulky feedstuffs, 173

Calcium, 73, 77
Carbohydrates, 56, 59
Carcase, 21
—, acceptability, 26
—, grade, 112
—, lean and fat, 111
Composition, 20
—, carcase, 21
—, faeces, 59
—, feeds, 59, 183, 184, 185
—, piglets, 26
—, sows, 38
Computer diet formulation, 163
Copper, 75, 176
Creep feed, 36, 166, 175

Diets for pigs, 166, 172
Diet, 154
—, density, 168
—, dilution, 90
—, formulation, 154, 159
—, ingredients, 155, 161, 183, 184
Digestible, 42
—, energy, 60, 156
—, nitrogen, 146
—, protein, 156, 183, 184
Digestibility, 41, 57
—, determination, 148
—, value of feedstuffs, 183, 184

Digestion, 41, 58
—, of energy, 57
—, of fats, 57
—, of minerals, 76
—, of protein, 41

Early weaning, 17, 34
Energy, 56
—, cost of fat deposition, 58, 61
—, cost of maintenance, 60
—, cost of protein deposition, 58, 61
—, digestibility, 58
—, efficiency of use, 61, 64, 67
—, for breeding sows, 127
—, for growth, 67
—, for lactation, 70
—, from protein, 63
—, for pregnancy, 68
—, in components of diet, 57
—, in components of growth, 58
—, in feedstuffs, 183, 184
—, metabolism, 60
—, protein interaction, 123

Fat, 59, 170
—, growth, 24
—, in feeds, 57, 183, 184
—, in meat, 20
—, mobilisation, 71, 130
Feed additives, 175
Feed formulation, 160
Feed intake, 89, 93, 115, 134
Feeding trials, 151
Feedstuffs, 145
—, chemical evaluation, 149
—, nutritive evaluation, 145, 151
—, nutritive value, 183, 184, 185
Fibre, 60, 153
Finisher diets, 166
Foetus, 31
—, losses, 33
Frequency of feeding, 92

Gilts, 30
—, puberty, 30
—, rationing, 140
Grazing, 152
Grower diets, 166
Growth, 22
—, compensatory, 50, 100, 174
—, conception products, 52

—, energy needs for, 67
—, fat, 25
—, foetus, 31
—, lean mass, 23
—, piglets, 37
—, promoters, 175
—, protein, 23
—, protein: fat, 26
—, protein needs for, 51
—, to maturity, 22
—, water in, 25

Heat treatment, 43
—, damage, 43
—, losses from body, 62
—, production, 65, 146
High density diets, 170
Hormones, 176

Individual feeding, 108
Ingredient restraints, 161, 183, 184

Joule, 57

Lactation, 34
—, energy needs, 70
—, protein needs, 54
—, rationing, 135
Lean growth, 24
—, meat, 20
Least-cost diets, 163, 169
Lysine, 40
—, essential amino acid, 45
—, in feedstuffs, 183, 184, 185
—, see also amino acids

Magnesium, 77
Maintenance, 60
—, energy, 61, 64, 68
—, protein, 51
Meat, 20
—, composition, 21
—, quality, 27
Metabolic body weight, 61, 182
—, faecal losses, 41
Metabolism crate, 147
—, study, 145
Methionine, see amino acids
Milk production, 34
—, composition, 71
—, energy costs, 70
—, from body fat, 71

Minerals, 73
—, deficiencies, 74
—, in body, 21, 73
—, requirements, 75
—, retention, 76
—, supplementation, 73

Nitrogen, 39, 146
Non-protein nitrogen, 48
Nutrient specification, 155
—, values, 168, 183, 184, 185

Ovulation, 31, 34

P_2 measurement, 112
Palatability, 145, 167, 175
Particle size, 42, 59
Pasture, 128, 152
Phosphorus, 76
Piglet composition, 26
—, diets, 166
Potassium, 76
Pregnancy, 30
—, anabolism, 53, 68
—, diets, 166
—, energy needs, 68
—, products, 31, 52
—, protein needs, 53
—, rationing, 101, 134
Protease inhibitors, 43
Protein, 39
—, for breeding sows, 127
—, deposition, 24, 114
—, digestion, 41
—, in diet, 119
—, in feedstuffs, 183, 184
—, in meat, 21
—, metabolism, 44
—, recycling, 44
—, requirements, 51, 53, 54
—, synthesis, 49
Puberty in boars, 27
—, in gilts, 30

Rationing, 93, 114
—, *ad lib*, 89, 93, 96
—, boars, 140
—, by time, 97
—, by weight, 96
—, pre-mating, 140
—, scales for growing pigs, 94, 110
—, sows, 101, 104, 108, 126, 142
Restraints, 161, 168, 183, 184

Salt, 76, 166
Sex, 24, 114
Slaughter weight, 119
Sodium, 76
Sow, 30
—, composition, 38
—, diets, 166
—, feeding, 101, 126
—, individuality, 129
Strain of pig, 24, 114, 121
Stress, 79, 91

Targets, 124
Temperature of body, 64
—, of environment, 64, 117, 128
—, lower critical, 65
Thin sow syndrome, 38
Threonine, *see amino acids*
Trace elements, 75
Trypsin inhibitors, 43

Vitamins, 78
—, deficiencies, 27, 78, 141
—, fat soluble, 79
—, requirements, 81
—, water soluble, 82

Water, 84
—, in body, 63
—, in meat, 21
—, requirements, 84
—, wet feeding, 86
Weight gain, 20
—, growing pigs, 26, 114
—, sow change, 107, 138
—, sow gain, 102
—, sow loss, 104

Yield of carcase, 21
—, of sperm, 27

Zinc, 75